SCAR TISSUE

lessons from the world of entrepreneurship

Daryl Erdman

Scar Tissue | Lessons from the World of Entrepreneurship

1st Edition Print 2010
Library of Congress Control Number: 2009939254

ISBN: 978-0-9819290-4-0

Editing by: Beth Bily
Book Design: Anthony Sclavi; BRIO LLC, Minneapolis, MN

Publishing & Distribution Agent: BRIO Press
Printed in the United States of America

Table of Contents

Acknowledgements

I believe it proper and fitting to list some of the people who directly and indirectly contributed to the writing of this book.

First, kudos have to go to my editor, Beth Bily, who exhibited much patience and understanding toward a fledging author in addition to helping make sense of an abundance of verbosity by showing how to write more precisely.

Of course, many thanks is belatedly due the late Msgr. Murphy, president of the University of

St. Thomas, who took the giant leap of offering a neophyte professor a chance to tackle something entirely new in business education.

The same thanks and acknowledgement must go to the wonderful faculty who helped us create two award winning collegiate programs in entrepreneurship followed by the hundreds of wonderful young student entrepreneurs who by their success helped us confirm the value of our education program.

Finally, I need to thank my wife, Audrey. You do not have a risk bone in your body, but have stuck by for 48 years through more change, risk assumption and leaps into the unknown than any conservative Norwegian deserves.

Foreword

In the early 1980s, the University of St. Thomas was one of the first universities to launch a Small Business and Entrepreneurship program. In filling the Chair, we were seeking a person with significant successful business experience to design our curriculum and teach the courses. Daryl Erdman excelled in this position.

As shown in this book, he has a unique ability to pull valuable insights from his business experiences, and state them in clear and forceful language. His ideas are sound, based on a healthy combination of practical experience and intellectual wisdom. Daryl's "scar tissue" experiences and the lessons learned from them will help everyone with entrepreneurial aspirations. This book is a must read for anyone who wants to be an entrepreneur, as well as anyone who is already fully engaged in one of the life-cycle stages of entrepreneurship.

Michael J Evers, PhD, Dean (Retired), Graduate School of Business, University of St. Thomas, Minneapolis, MN

Preface

"The hardest thing to learn in life is which bridge to cross and which...to burn"
David Russell

Scar tissue events are the result of errors in judgment. Singly, such events most often result in a recoverable setback. In the extreme, and when compounded, they can cause failure of an entrepreneurial venture. Most of these mistakes are totally avoidable given a little more time or due diligence. However, being human, we all tend to make more mistakes than necessary.

Before beginning this project I took time to Google books on the general topic of entrepreneurship. I found 5.5 million entries! As I refined my search, I found about 2 million on the subject of entrepreneurial failure. That number was further winnowed to about 228,000 on "pitfalls."

When I began developing a collegiate entrepreneurial program in 1983 I believe I could have counted the number of scholarly works about entrepreneurship on my fingers. So, why would I think that one more book would contribute anything that has not already been written? What could I possibly bring to the discussion that would be creative and new, especially in view of the turbulent economic times in which we now live?

Now, when inflation is low, interest cost down, space is readily available and relatively cheap, when most businesses that were once formidable competitors are struggling and unemployment is high with loads of talent looking for work, this should be an ideal time for the entrepreneur to launch his/her "dream" business.

If we look at history, which I am prone to do, we find that recessionary times have produced 16 of 30 companies that comprise the Dow Industrial Average - companies like Proctor and Gamble, Johnson & Johnson, Disney, General Electric and McDonalds. Perhaps tough times reduce the personal risk assessment of entrepreneurs, and foster a "what is there to lose?" attitude.

There are those who would argue that today's times are different but I believe little has changed. Financial markets have tightened, there is the potential for higher taxes and venture capital is reassessing its role. In short, that precious resource called money is in short supply. Times like these can cause a winnowing effect where only the strongest survive. However, on the positive side, this also means fewer startups competing for the most precious resource of all, people.

There is certainly opportunity now but at the same time we all have witnessed where greed has taken us. For many, a personal reassessment of the type of business leaders we wish to emulate and follow is warranted.

The principled and ethical entrepreneur can step into this chasm. Currently, cash is the only scarce, necessary resource. It is time to reexamine how one can go about constructing a viable entity without an excessive amount of it. I often have found that the struggle to build an enterprise with scarce resources leads to even greater long-term success than one started with an abundance of resources.

So, what is unique about this undertaking? What makes it relevant today? What will this book bring to the table that might help someone avoid a serious pitfall and achieve success?

This work's contribution is likely subtle. It offers unique perspective from my own varied career along with lessons from countless entrepreneurs that I have had the privilege of teaching, mentoring and investing in along the way. It is my hope that avoiding more serious "scar tissue" lessons will help the entrepreneur become even more successful. At the very least, this little bit of foreknowledge might help avert fatal error.

Many entrepreneurial works are rooted in the assumption that somehow one can follow the critical "12 Steps to Success as an Entrepreneur" and have success assured. While there are critical and necessary steps to be followed, these are not always the same. For every established step or rule, I have found a successful entrepreneur who is the exception. This even includes the "holy grail" of writing a business plan. This work may seem at times to glide over accepted practices. Its intended purpose is not that of definitive tutorial, but rather avoiding pitfalls. Perhaps the subtitle could have been "Lessons in Common Sense."

Once the decision to share some of the scar tissue events that I have either been involved in directly or have witnessed, I needed to decide how I wished to organize the book so that it wasn't just a collection of war stories that may or may not be of benefit to the reader. Having spent about 45 years of my life connected in some way to the practice of entrepreneurship I reflected on the nuances of the journey itself.

It has been my experience that entrepreneurial events, even the better ones with great teams of people, usually start with a single individual and an idea. Thus, the first section of the book is devoted to that individual. In these early stages, stress is extremely high, fear of failure and self-doubt abound, pressure to perfect the product/service is paramount and urgency to find money is mounting. I creatively decided to call this first section "The Entrepreneur."

From the entrepreneur, the issues of startup are tackled in the second section titled, "From Initiation to Birth." This section deals with the frustrating time of pulling together a team, a plan and finding financing to move the idea forward. Here, there is pressure to maintain and preserve cash, initiate some form of company structure, add policies and procedures, and figure out ways to develop sales momentum.

Section three, "Survival and Growth," addresses the metamorphic transitions needed to help achieve a modicum of success. Competitive issues begin to arise and the entrepreneurial venture needs to formally develop a management culture, integrate people, strategically plan, enhance management systems, and perhaps find additional resources.

This metamorphic change then continues into section four, "From Sustainability to Immortality." As the entrepreneur moves into a stage where success is assured, an enduring entity begins to evolve. The issues faced at this stage are developing, then formalizing, more complex management and operational systems. The venture can no longer be managed in a "hands-on" style so better delegation will be required. Stress will stem from issues such as; staying focused and involved, the need for better people management and the challenge of maintaining the critical culture.

Finally the entrepreneurial creation will reach a stage I have called, "Final Maturity, Separation and Legacy," which, with luck, will be where the creation and the entrepreneur will come to successful conclusion. In this section, I address a variety of scar tissue issues - everything from avoiding an ending with failure to trying to overstay one's ability to be effective.

Introduction

"Many a man never fails because he never tries"
Norman MacEwan

For as long as I can remember I have had an independent streak and a desire to carve out my own destiny. Early on, I never equated this with being entrepreneurial but rather with a feeling that it would be more challenging and interesting to rely on my own abilities.

I had the wonderful opportunity to both practice being an entrepreneur (I say practice because very few can perfect it) and develop two collegiate programs that taught it. I spent 23 years developing seven different businesses, then another 15 years as an academic. My career culminated with a short stint as a professional venture capitalist, which helped me gain further insight.

In the teaching phase of my career, I often told students that as one "practices" the career of entrepreneurship, mistakes along the way would result in the build up of "scar tissue." Experience has shown that good entrepreneurs learn from scar tissue and hone their skills to become continuously better at starting and growing organizations from ideas. (I use the term organizations rather than businesses because there are almost as many non-profit entrepreneurs as for-profit ones. In addition there are the "intrepreneurs," a term that Gifford Pinchot coined in 1985 with his seminal work, Intrepreneuring, or people who create a new entity within an existing organizational setting.)

Through my exposure, both vicariously and personally, I often watched people trip themselves, making the same mistakes as others who had gone before. I kept thinking that an attempt to record some of the more obvious pitfalls could serve as a warning and a lesson for new entrepreneurs - saving time, money and angst.

There are those who will argue that experience is the best teacher. When he was alive, a friend and fellow instructor of entrepreneurship, Dr. Jeff Timmons of Babson College, observed that one could measure the quality of the entrepreneur by the depth of scar tissue. In other words, those able to survive and overcome early mistakes usually made better entrepreneurs. While this may be true, my hope is to shorten the learning curve.

A considerable amount of my research consists of personal experience, seasoned with mentoring approximately 76 student-developed businesses over 15 years. I also benefited from knowing multiple entrepreneurs, who helped me gain from their experience.

For the past 10 years, I also have written a small advice column titled, The Business Mentor, published monthly in a wonderful little business newspaper in the upper Midwest, BusinessNorth. Wayne Nelson, editor and publisher, has patiently and graciously allowed me to put my thoughts about entrepreneurs, entrepreneurship and business development to paper. This experience has helped me sort out my own philosophy while sharing collective entrepreneurial scar tissue. This accumulation of columns will allow me to draw upon what I have written and perhaps, with some editing and embellishment, pull these ideas and thoughts together in a more logical presentation. I also have gained further knowledge of "scar tissue events" through the wonderful contacts that have come about because of the column.

Section One: The Entrepreneur

"It is never too late to be
who you might have been."
George Eliot

Chapter One

What Defines an Entrepreneur?

Early Choices

The question of what constitutes an entrepreneur really bedeviled me when I began teaching the discipline at St. Thomas University in 1984. I had not given any thought to the subject when I began my own entrepreneurial career. In fact, I am not even sure I knew how to spell the word much less define it.

I started my career in a family business right after receiving my MBA from Michigan State University in

1962. It was not an easy decision. It meant turning down several unique and exciting (not to mention better paying) job opportunities. One opportunity was particularly intriguing - it involved travel in South America, working for the Kennedy Administration's Food for Peace Program. Those who accepted the positions worked with local business people to develop U.S. style supermarkets in rural areas. A pilot project had been successful and for a young, eager and very green MBA this opportunity seemed exciting.

While there was intriguing possibility, reality played a larger role in my early career decisions. I had a pregnant wife, no money, bills to pay and a family business calling. I went to work in the family four-store supermarket chain started by my grandfather in 1925. I was determined to grow the business for a couple of reasons. One motivator was obvious - we needed a larger business to support the five families involved. The second was more personal - I needed to test my own abilities.

Early Lessons

I would have never defined this "itch" as "entrepreneurship" in those days. To me, it was just an independent streak, which made joining the family business harder, but a decision I made after assurances came that I would be able to lead development and expansion. I never gave a thought to being an entrepreneur. I just felt that starting and building a business from scratch would be the ultimate challenge. I soon had secured the lease rights to a new supermarket, which was to be an anchor in a new shopping center well within our trade area. After about a year's work, the family outvoted my vision and the new store was turned down.

I was temporarily deflated and resigned from the family business to go about developing the store on my own. I was soon to gain some of my first scar tissue and lose the "MBA chip on the shoulder."

My first objective was financing. I had $5,000 in assets and required financing of more than $250,000. It almost goes without saying that the banker had a good laugh. However, he did step in and arranged for developers to do the financing and amortize it over the length of my lease. When it came to staffing, what I thought would be easy was not. I was unable to attract any experienced talent. I ended up with only two veterans and about 50 totally inexperienced workers. This dilemma was addressed through the development of training programs and requiring employees to work with pay one hour past closing for training. It took the first year before the store ran smoothly. While this early venture had its setbacks, it paled in comparison to the scar tissue that was to come.

A few years later I, along with a very good friend with extensive radio experience, decided we would start a radio station. In our attempt to secure a Federal Communications Commission license we found out that the process, at that time, would take approximately two years. When we discovered that an FCC license wasn't required to start a network, our plan shifted.

We did some quick market surveying, calling a wide range of rural stations in Minnesota to assess need for additional programming. It turned out that there was nearly unanimous desire to receive national news along with local university and professional sports programs.

Based on this feedback, we developed our concept. We were fortunate to obtain rights to a national news feed from a leading Minneapolis market station and secured rights to broadcast University of Minnesota sports. We also won approval to broadcast the major professional team sports in the state. All this came before the advent of modern communication ability, so we needed to reach agreement with AT&T to provide hard-wired phone lines between each station and us. It was a difficult negotiation, but we were able to pull it off.

Financing was our next obstacle. We decided to arrange financing from a group of investors in three tranches. We then set objectives to be met before investment would have to be made. This approach made raising capital a little easier. We raised the first round and were making progress toward clearing the first hurdle for a second round; securing contractual arrangements with 22 rural radio stations in our broadcast area.

Based upon our projections, we needed 22 stations on board to ensure viability. We decided that, in order to facilitate this process, we would bring in a general manager and put him on the road to sell the concept to stations. The individual we hired had worked in the radio business in our area for many years. We both knew him, so did not bother with any vetting. In short order, the new manager had secured 12 contracts and things were looking up. The date for our next investor meeting and the second round of financing was fast approaching, when suddenly securing additional contracts became a challenge.

With 10 days to go, I proposed we delay the meeting, realizing we were still stuck on the initial count of 12 contracts. The interest seemed strong enough that, given a little more time, we should be able to meet our goal. Our manager, however, insisted we go ahead. At the meeting, he brought

24 contracts signed sealed and delivered! It was amazing - all of the investors immediately wrote checks for the next round.

Elation was short-lived. As I drove back to my office, I went over the meeting in my mind - an uneasy feeling building. Upon returning, I called my partner and asked him what he thought. He said he also had reservations and was about to call me. I called our manager and told him I was coming back.

When I arrived, I found our receptionist in his office in tears and upon seeing me, she confessed that the manager had forced her to forge all the new contracts. I was astonished and angry all at the same time. I immediately fired the manager and called my partner. That evening we decided to return all of the investment and shut the operation down. It was a deep financial blow, which left us with a greater appreciation for the importance of doing in-depth background checks on people with whom much authority and responsibility is placed. One dishonest individual single-handedly brought down what otherwise could have been a very successful endeavor.

As painful as this scar tissue was to obtain, it was no more painful than others acquired over my lifetime. Fortunately, none of the missteps I made were fatal career choices and all served me well as future lessons, both in business and academia.

While my early mistakes were recoverable, it is precisely these early lessons that prompted this work. It is my hope that others can learn from these and other examples before making the same mistakes.

Defining what it Means to be an Entrepreneur

Prior to enumerating the pitfalls experienced by entrepreneurs, it is useful to explore what constitutes an entrepreneur.

There are many definitions of the entrepreneur, but not many upon which there is common agreement. I am not sure it is critically important. I do know that many early pioneers in entrepreneurial education, myself included, struggled to find a definition. I believe that we came close when we recognized that an entrepreneur was someone who pursued an opportunity without regard for the capital requirements to implement it. This definition was broad enough to encompass almost any type of individual pursuit to develop an idea from start to finish.

There are several kinds of entrepreneurs and entrepreneurial events. There are, what I have termed, lifestyle entrepreneurs, who wish to have just enough success to maintain a certain lifestyle.

The income replacement entrepreneur has a developed skill and wishes to work by him/herself and replace the income previously earned by working for someone else.

The "empire builder" loves to build and relishes the competitive battle of becoming the best at his/her trade. Richard Schultz of the Best Buy Company and Bill Gates of Microsoft are examples of empire builders.

Finally, there is the "serial entrepreneur." This is a person who creates multiple entities over a lifetime. This entrepreneur enjoys the thrill and challenge of pursuing an idea to the point of success, but soon becomes bored when success is achieved. Moving on to other events will re-energize this individual. Bruce Thomson, who at the ripe age of 70 began a fast pizza food concept, can be included in this group. Thomson is currently somewhere around his twelfth startup (about six successes and six failures). His successes have been spectacular - companies like Pemtom (a housing developer with over 6,000 homes built), Proex Photo, Title Wave, and the Archiver's chain. Manny Villafana, who has founded six medical companies, including Cardiac Pacemakers, St. Jude and Helix BioCore, also fits this category.

Entrepreneurs are not only found in the business world. People such as former priest, Joe Selvaggio, who built the nonprofit, Project for Pride in Living, in the inner city of Minneapolis easily can be defined as an entrepreneur. Starting from scratch out of his parish, he began to utilize the skills of his parishioners to rehab abandoned houses for the underprivileged. From this point, it grew into a very successful community non-profit entity, which has a budget of several million dollars, employs several hundred people and provides housing, jobs and education to disadvantaged people in the inner city.

I would argue that all of the above could rightfully claim the title of entrepreneur. Anyone who can recognize an idea and pursue it through to build an organization around it to serve a market or a community certainly has claim to succeeding in an entrepreneurial event.

After 23 years and developing seven different business ventures, I transitioned to academia at the University of St. Thomas in St. Paul, Minnesota. I accepted an endowed position as "Professor of Entrepreneurship and Small Business." Almost immediately I learned how to spell "entrepreneurship." The question was: Could it be taught? I also pondered who would be the students of this new discipline?

After much thought and several failed attempts, I came to the conclusion that no other profession attempted to pre-determine who fit within its curriculum. Why should entrepreneurship be any different?

Through a program of courses, students would learn what it took to start a business and then be able to decide for themselves if it was something they wished to pursue. This necessitated that courses be taught by people who had, at least one time in their lives, met their own payrolls. In other words, the faculty needed to be entrepreneurs in their own right. They had to have walked the walk, so to speak.

My academic antagonists were not satisfied; many felt that this program and its approach were too applied. They wanted a more esoteric, academic approach to the program. Naturally, I disagreed. Entrepreneurship study and pursuit is a professional endeavor and, like any profession, the graduates had the right to assume that the skills they were taught would allow them to actually start a business.

Jeff Timmons from Babson College, a past leader in entrepreneurial education, once said that it takes "144 bits of knowledge to be a successful entrepreneur." (This was an arbitrary number Timmons selected to illustrate that one must be reasonably good at many different skills in order to build a successful enterprise. It is, nonetheless, useful as a concept.)

Certainly a job with a narrow focus within a large company does little to help in the acquisition of that knowledge. Age and experience can aid people in becoming more successful as long as the experience comes from being an entrepreneur. But, youth, combined with the proper qualities, also has proven time and again to be a formula for success.

Entrepreneurs and Nature versus Nurture

Many academics claim that entrepreneurs are born and not made, so naturally it would do little good to try to teach it. My counter: The musical prodigy also is born with innate gifts, but still needs to be taught, mentored, developed and encouraged to practice.

The approach that many instructors of this new discipline took was not unlike any other academic pursuit. Skills that are necessary to becoming a successful entrepreneur were assessed, and then courses were created to teach those skills.

Entrepreneurship requires hard skills, such as knowing and understanding of the basics of marketing with minimal resources, some understanding of the legal issues involved, financing, financial projections and cash flow management. As an instructor, I also devoted time to company formation, looking at softer management skills and developing company cultures. Coursework culminated with business plan development. In addition to skills, we studied successful entrepreneurial events and invited many of those successful entrepreneurs to either teach or speak to students.

Although defining what we were to teach presented challenges, after the program was launched, we found success. Students at both the graduate and undergraduate level loved it. In less than 10 years, entrepreneurship became a nationally recognized course of business study. We had become a full department at St. Thomas - our own undergraduate major with approximately 200 students enrolled along with an MBA concentration with another 200 students. We tracked 76 student-started businesses, which were running at better than a 90 percent success rate. Two of the students had already sold their first businesses for more than $40 million each.

Through trial and error, we were able to develop courses that were helpful to people beginning an entrepreneurial career, adding weight to the argument that it is not all simply genetic.

Some of the early teaching material reminded me of a comic strip from Fox Trot by Bill Amend. In this particular segment the father wants to start his own business and sends away for a self-help guide. When the guide arrives, he finds the three easy steps inside: "Step 1—Create a product to see for $200. Step 2—Get 5,000 people to buy it. Step 3—Uncork the champagne, you're now a millionaire!"

I would hope that the majority of those reading this already are aware that attempting to follow such a simple guideline would be a sure way of achieving failure, not success. The process of developing a successful venture is much more detailed and involved. A successful business is much like a three-legged stool. The legs represent opportunity, people and capital. With any one of these elements missing, the stool will not stand and neither will a business.

Yet we found many skeptics about this so-called new business discipline called "entrepreneurship" in the early days. Some said this new academic discipline model was working because we "hand-selected" people who would probably have become successful entrepreneurs on their own (the old "nature" theme). Encouragement and some "special training" simply enhanced success, said doubters.

There are still authors today who question the authenticity of entrepreneurship and entrepreneur programs.

Joseph Schumpeter (one of the few economists to ever write about the entrepreneurial phenomena) asserted it was the risk taker who brought forward new products and services. The creative destruction that entrepreneurs bring to the marketplace makes free markets vibrant, he says. He also distinguishes between inventor and innovator. He argues the innovator (and I believe one could substitute the word entrepreneur here) takes a new idea or product and produces it efficiently and profitably.

A work by Tom Harrison, Instinct (Grand Central Publishing, 2006), argues that we are hard-wired through our DNA to be entrepreneurs. Harrison is the CEO of Omnicom DAS and a former cell biologist who claims to have developed a test that can tell if one is "born to win as an entrepreneur." Harrison says that there are five personality traits that make the entrepreneur. These traits are: openness to new experiences, conscientiousness, extroversion, agreeableness and neuroticism.

There are, in my mind, problems with using trait theory as an indicator of entrepreneurial success. The same traits that breed entrepreneurial success also bring success to those in most any field.

But, not all experts view entrepreneurship as a solely innate gift.

In the book, Talent is Never Enough by John Maxwell (Thomas Nelson, Inc., 2007), the author describes in detail some of the qualities that need to be honed and developed for a successful entrepreneurial undertaking. Dr. Maxwell is a leading author on leadership, recognized worldwide for his training programs and books, which have sold more than 12 million copies.

Maxwell argues that it is critical to believe in oneself, one's potential and one's mission. He says that belief needs to stimulate action, followed by results. Talented people must possess passion for that which they wish to accomplish along with the initiative it takes to make it happen.

Maxwell expands further on the need for focus, preparation, practice and the need to enlist others in order to achieve ultimate success. The ability to recognize one's strengths and weaknesses and find corresponding talent in others is vital. Building a successful team can be one of most important building blocks to further success. To attract this talent is never easy yet, example after example abounds of successful organizations whose leaders have been able to do just that.

A second book with like perspective is, Go Put Your Strengths To Work, by Marcus Buckingham, (Free Press, 2007). Buckingham was formerly with the Gallup Organization (yes the famous pollsters), whose major activity is in the field of management training. Buckingham is a well-known author whose previous works came out of the research he did while at Gallup on the world's best leaders and managers. This book dovetails nicely with Maxwell's and also with Buckingham's previous work, Now, Discover Your Strengths.

Buckingham is a leading proponent of discovering, then developing, the strengths of individuals while ignoring their weaknesses. It is his contention that too much time in management education is spent focusing on people's weaknesses and then trying to change or improve them. He believes that working with and expanding a person's strengths will net far better results.

The previously discussed survey of works on this topic leads me to this conclusion: The successful entrepreneur is likely a blend of nature and nurture. There are many entrepreneurial lessons that can be taught, but I must add that inherent qualities can separate the successful entrepreneur. One critical talent needed is the ability to deal with ambiguity - discussed further in the next section, "Adaptors and Innovators." The vast majority of our students who opted out of the program did so because of an inability to work with constant ambiguity. Ambiguity is inherent in any entrepreneurial event; by its very nature, a venture is unstructured.

Adaptors and Innovators

My associate director at the University of St. Thomas, Dr. Rajiv Tandon, discovered the work of a London-based psychologist, Dr. Michael Kirton, who developed a simple psychometric measure called the Kirton Adaption-Innovation Inventory. After Tandon became trained in this instrument, we employed it in our program and tested every student upon entering. On a continuum, this instrument measures the way people think, show creativity, solve problems and make decisions. The results are reported on a scale from extreme adaptor to extreme innovator. This can best be shown in the comparison that follows:

Characteristics of Adaptors and Innovators

Adaptors

- Safe, reliable, methodical
- Disciplined and efficient seen as irrelevant masters details for overview
- Prefers defined problems
- Rarely challenges the rules; despite a rule
- Seeks consensus , values group cohesion
- Does things better
- Provides balance when working with innovator

Innovators

· Thinks in risky, unexpected ways

· Little respect for past custom-seen as irrelevant

· Trades off detail for overview

· Questions definition of problem

· Often challenges the problems despite a rule

· Can appear insensitive, even abrasive

· Does things differently

This was a wonderful and non-judgmental instrument for our program. It simply describes how one goes about thinking, problem solving, adjusting to rules, policy and forming consensus. Of course, there are shortcomings at the extremes of both scales.

Our use of the scale confirmed Kirton's discovery that the highly adaptive personality could see absolutely no shortcomings to their working style while the highly creative could readily cite issues. The highly creative also report that, in spite of the issues, they simply do not care what others think.

The two opposing styles have trouble working together but really can be more effective as a team - if they are able to understand the other style and develop a tolerance for it. Innovators will find adaptors overly protective of the status quo - too concerned with following the rules and essentially "boring." However, without adaptors very little would get accomplished. Conversely, the innovator's disregard of rules at times is necessary. The free flow of ideas can be stimulating and the willingness to try new things is essential to any organization's ability to adapt and stay viable.

In the years we employed Kirton's instrument in our program, we became convinced that it was difficult for an extreme innovator to carry off a successful entrepreneurial event on his/her own. Very simply, the continuous flow of new ideas would prove to be a distraction, making it difficult to stay focused long enough to accomplish goals. We also found that the high adaptors would most likely drop out of our program primarily because the total ambiguity of entrepreneurship would drive the desire for orderliness and rule-following to the point of utter frustration.

Although our database was most likely insufficient to draw any definitive conclusions, we were able to come to some "unproven" conclusions. First, we found that our better entrepreneurs fell from the middle of the scale to leaning a little bit toward the innovative side. Our high innovators had distinct problems with keeping the intensive focus that was needed to bring an opportunity to successful implementation. We also found that even people who fell within the preferable parameters of Kirton's scale greatly benefited when teamed with someone higher on the adaptive scale.

Overall, the instrument served both instructors and students very well when it came to assisting in team selection and team building for new ventures.

How Often Do Businesses Fail? And Nature versus Nurture

I do need to dispel some false statistics about the failure rate of new ventures. What's Stopping You, authors Bruce R. Barringer and R. Duane Ireland (FT Press, 2008) quote from credible data that 66 percent of new businesses are still operating after two years, 50 percent survive for four years or more and 40 percent survive for six years or more. The authors also note that about one-third of businesses that close or are sold are still considered to be successful by their owners.

There is no such thing as an entrepreneurial gene that predisposes a person to business ownership, say Barringer and Ireland. One can learn from the failures of others and overcome self-limiting behaviors to increase the odds of success. The book is a good read for the aspiring entrepreneur, offering encouragement and offsetting the perceived risk of starting a business by measuring that risk against the risks of a corporate career.

A Model for Entrepreneurial Leadership

Now that we have loosely defined the entrepreneur and some personality traits and their relationship to the entrepreneur have been discussed, it is important to note that the skills needed in a venture fluctuate as it matures.

There is a body of research on the various stages that an organization will go through as it passes from birth to maturity. There is great necessity for flexibility and adaptability in the entrepreneur's managerial style. We will treat this in greater detail in later, but for now it is important to recognize that in order to see a beginning organization all the way to final success, its founder will need to change and adapt his/her leadership style.

The need for changed leadership is underscored by the changing needs of each stage of the venture's development. Much like a child, an organization will move through the following stages in its development.

Stage I (Birth)

- · Shared Tasks
- · Euphoria
- · Excitement
- · High Energy
- · Sleepless nights

Stage II (Early Childhood)

- · Many new things to learn
- · Mistakes made
- · Lessons learned
- · Constant demands
- · Conflicting demands
- · Constant change
- · Reactionary

Stage III (Teen Years)

- · Pride in what has been produced
- · Frustration when things don't go as planned
- · Guidelines and policies should be structured and followed
- · Roles need to be defined
- · Freedoms and delegation need to evolved

Stage IV (Early Adult)

· Begin to enjoy the fruits of labor

· More coaching and monitoring

· Systems in place

· More leisure time

Stage V (Adult)

· Final harvest: perhaps grandchildren

· Expansions, mergers and acquisitions

Eric Flamholtz, a professor of management at UCLA, wrote a book titled, How to Make the Transition from an Entrepreneurship to a Professionally Managed Firm (Jossey-Bass Publishers, 1986). In it, he utilizes a pyramid as a metaphor for a company's development.

Flamholtz's pyramid begins with:

· Identifying and defining a market niche

· Developing products and services

· Acquiring resources

· Developing operational systems

· Developing management systems

· Developing a corporate culture.

I like the logical sequence laid out in this work. Although things in real life do not always follow such an orderly progression, this process outline is a good one to model. The order of this book follows Flatholtz's pyramid to a great extent.

Pre-Scar Tissue Event

Fear of the Open Kimono
"This is such a Great Idea that I Can't Tell Anybody!"

When defining opportunity, a first "pre" scar tissue event can kill the opportunity before it gets to first base. When an idea is first identified it is important to take time to "talk it around." This means sharing the idea with essentially anyone who will listen. Asking questions about what people think and really listening to feedback will enable fine-tuning.

Openness and total honesty is the best policy here. It is not unlike a first-time physical when the doctor tells the patient to take off all clothing. The patient, undoubtedly, is uncomfortable at the prospect of standing naked in front of a stranger. Afterward, there is realization that it was not so bad and there are certainly health benefits that come from the process. The same is true for a venture idea.

Unfortunately, many people cannot get past the

initial fear of sharing an idea. Much of that fear, of course, is rooted in the belief that the idea will be stolen. I will not deny there is some risk when sharing ideas with others. I had it happen to me with one venture and I also saw it happen to a student. If one is, in fact, first with an idea and someone else hears about it, then tweaks it enough to circumvent early proprietary protection in order to compete, it can be an early devastating blow.

My experience has shown that, in general, these cases tend to be in the minority and do not happen as often as one might expect. Assuming the idea is unique; someone attempting to copy will never have the same passion as the originator. This drive will sustain most ventures through many of the early trials and pitfalls. Executing a venture with better precision and expertise will lower the odds of being bested if copying attempts are made.

Assessing Personal Strengths and Weaknesses

The entrepreneur must move beyond simply understanding his/her personality on the Kirton scale. Honesty about ability will help build self-awareness, which many feel is critical for long-term entrepreneurial success. I have always believed that successful entrepreneurs exhibit "entrepreneurial leadership" versus the more traditional textbook management style of organizational control. I will deal with that in more depth later. In the meantime, I would suggest budding entrepreneurs add, What Got You Here Won't Get You There, by Marshall Goldsmith, (Hyperion, 2007) to their reading list. Goldsmith, a famous management consultant/trainer, helps business leaders achieve personal change. The work outlines 21 interpersonal habits that can block leadership success.

The critical importance of being able to identify personal strengths and weaknesses in order to build a successful team (and thus achieve total entrepreneurial success) can be easier said than done. Goldsmith goes into detail about specific behavioral issues that are problematic and how to correct them. Personally identifying the things that are problematic is always difficult at best. This outline makes it easier to identify those issues that were not previously perceived as troublesome.

The 21 interpersonal habits the author addresses are:

· Winning too much

· Adding too much value

· Passing judgment

· Making destructive comments

· Starting with "NO" "BUT" or "HOWEVER"

· Telling the world how smart we are

· Speaking when angry

· Negativity, or "Let me explain why that won't work"

· Withholding information

· Failing to give proper recognition

· Claiming credit that we don't deserve

· Making excuses

· Clinging to the past

· Playing favorites

· Refusing to express regret

· Not listening

· Failing to express gratitude

· Punishing the messenger

· Passing the buck

· An excessive need to be "ME;" and

· Goal obsession (this last one is not so much a flaw as it is the cause of overlooking the larger mission)

Just listing the 21 items will not be of much help, but hopefully the list might be intriguing enough to warrant further exploration. Personal flaws can impede success and even cause failure.

Filling the Knowledge Gap

Understanding personal strengths and weaknesses, further development of strengths and working on correcting behavioral issues that can impede success will go a long way toward achieving entrepreneurial success. There also are times when the entrepreneur is missing knowledge integral to the opportunity. Finding missing knowledge up front is vital before progressing. One way this can be achieved is by locating an organization that may have the missing piece or pieces needed to round out the "144 bits of knowledge" key to success. Then, one must secure a job, either voluntary or paid, with that organization.

Let me give an example:

I had a student named John who absolutely loved to ski and wanted to find an opportunity near a major ski area. He decided to open a coffee house in Telluride, Colorado. At the time, this was a relatively new ski area and the town had no coffee shops. The problems were that John knew nothing about coffee and he had no money.

I was able to arrange an internship with a regional coffee roasting company and John spent part of his junior and senior years in this unpaid internship. He learned everything he could about coffee. He also learned about a famous quote from Yogi Berra, "You can observe a lot by just watching." Upon graduation John called me over to his car in the parking lot and in the U-Haul trailer, attached to his car, was a very nice coffee espresso machine, which the coffee company had loaned him to launch his business.

He headed to Telluride and found roommates in some fellow skiers. One was a good carpenter who built John a street cart for his espresso machine. A local bakery made his pastries. Over the summer he made enough money to rent some retail space close to the ski area. His new venture fared well until one day a New York executive who had recently moved to Telluride announced that he was opening a high-end coffee shop.

I advised John to sit down and have a conversation with this individual, which he did. As it turned out, John's potential competitor was a career coffee broker. The end result was that the two formed a partnership and went on to develop multiple locations in various ski areas around Colorado. They also went on to build their own roasting facility to develop custom blends for themselves and provide wholesale coffee to high-end restaurants.

John later sold his interest to his partner and spent a year traveling to every coffee growing country in the world to learn even more about coffee. He returned to become a specialty coffee consultant. This all came about because of his willingness to not allow a knowledge gap to keep him from pursuing his dream opportunity. (And, yes, he did get to ski a lot.)

John, although he did not know it at the time, followed the advice Dr. Randy Pausch, the Carnegie Mellon University professor, outlined in his famous "Last Lecture" - One must take risks in order to really live.

Pausch's lecture has much to say about entrepreneurship. He spoke at length about pursuing and accomplishing a dream, deciding early in life whether one is a Tigger (optimist) or an Eeyore (pessimist), working hard to become good at something and being prepared. He added that "luck" is where preparation meets opportunity and when one does the right thing, good stuff has a way of happening. He offers key points on enlisting the help of others:

· You can't go there alone and I believe in Karma

· Tell the truth

· Be earnest

· Apologize when you screw up

· Focus on others and not yourself

· Focus on people and learning to work in groups

· Get people to tell you what you need to hear by developing a feedback loop...and listen!

· Show gratitude

·· Don't complain...work harder

The Last Lecture is more than worth the time any reader (or viewer) will invest. It can be found on YouTube as mentioned above or simply go to: www.cmu.edu/randyslecture.

Assessing Strengths and Weaknesses in the Venture

The would-be entrepreneur should not stop at assessing personal strengths and weaknesses but go on to do the same for the proposed venture. This is all part of the "open kimono" perspective needed. Assess all the risks that could impact success.

The "Universe of Risk" encompasses all that anyone associated with a new venture will ask or, the at very least, have in the back of their minds. More than cursory thought is required here to furnish a reasonable assessment upon inquiry.

Business Partners

How have confidentiality and non-competitive issues been handled?

Competitive Situation

What will be the reaction to a new entry? Can competitive advantage be maintained and for how long? How accurate is competitive intelligence and niche identification, how was this determined?

Customer

What about product liability and customer credit risk? What is the market timing for customer purchase decisions? Has the venture worked through order fulfillment, guaranty and warranty issues?

Distribution

Will this be adequate, have the capacity and be able to provide speed of service? What about the cost? How will packaging be done? How dependable is all of this?

Financial

What is the timeline to positive cash flow and eventual profitability? Is this reasonable? Can positive cash flow be reached in 12 to 24 months, achieve after-tax profitability of 10 to 15 percent, and reach an investment return of 25 to 30 percent in five years? Is the amount of capital required to do this reasonable (under $1 million)?

Operational

Are contractual relationships covered satisfactorily? What about equipment needs? If successful, is capacity adequate? How will internal processes and controls be set up?

Political and Regulatory

Can intellectual property rights be enforced? Is the venture legally covered in this matter? Have all regulatory and economic issues been considered? Are there any potential changes in any of these that can impact the venture? Have all required licenses, environmental compliances, and regulatory approvals been acquired?

Technological

How complex is the product/service to develop? Can this cause delays or other related issues? Will the product or service become obsolete rapidly? Are requisite skill sets, ability and experience in place?

This is by no means an exhaustive list but meant only to illustrate the wide spectrum of critical risks.

Risk Assessment

We do need to speak to the entire issue of risk for the entrepreneur. To the general public, the risks entrepreneurs seem to be taking present overwhelming and huge obstacles. The whole idea of leaving the comfort of a secure job with benefits and plunging into something new and unstructured is an anathema. Entrepreneurs are viewed much like high stake gamblers plunging in without a safety net.

Risk is something that is a critical part of entrepreneurship. Without risk assumption, I would doubt many new businesses would ever be started. I would bet that if time were spent speaking to the average person on the street he/she would almost unanimously agree that "risk taker" would be part and parcel of the description of an entrepreneur. Yet in study after study it has been shown that most entrepreneurs are risk adverse. They go out of the way to avoid or minimize it.

Smart entrepreneurs always consciously or unconsciously assess the risk of whatever it is that they are planning to do. They will attempt to limit it through some of the following methodologies:

· Weigh the upside versus the downside and work to find ways to increase the former and limit the latter. Spread investment over more partners so each will have less to lose. Rented, borrowed, or contracted assistance will reduce the amount of money needed.

· Advance sales can jump-start the business and secure much needed cash flow.

· Alternative distribution strategies can save overhead. Example: A student who started a frozen food business was able to utilize a major frozen pizza distributor to deliver his product.

· Work with suppliers to obtain extended initial credit terms. Example: In one of my own start-ups, I was able to negotiate initial opening inventory from a key vendor. I agreed that cash would be paid for all new orders beyond the initial order if he would allow me to pay for the initial order over a 90-day period.

· Forge alliances; be creative. One entrepreneur I knew needed to have products designed in order to launch his business. He hired design engineers to moonlight to do this job. He paid them with a percentage of sales of the products they designed - an incentive for them to do a good job.

Many entrepreneurs evaluate risk by balancing best and worst-case scenarios. If assessment shows a much heavier weighting toward the best case they will most likely go for it even though the public would most likely view any worst-case possibility not worth the risk.

The entrepreneur must always look at the worst case and place one more strike against it – the time required to recover. During youth, it is easier to assume greater risk because, even after total failure, there is ample time to recover and, in the meantime, gain nearly a lifetime of experience.

Risk to the entrepreneur is somewhat relative, but, nonetheless, daunting. A very successful entrepreneurial friend of mine once put this in perspective. He said, looking out over the parking lot of his plant from his third floor window, "Every time I look over this parking lot I think about the fact that I am responsible for about 350 car payments."

Risk Assessment and Betting the Farm – Two Stories

I once had a friend who owned a company by the name of Minnetonka Corporation. He started the company by sub-contracting home workers to roll soap into decorative balls for sale in specialty gift retail shops. Since he was very creative, he soon saw opportunity to market liquid soap in a pump container for hand washing. The brand "Soft Soap" was developed.

As a small company, he soon was faced with competition from major manufacturers. His sales began to suffer and he sold the brand to Colgate-Palmolive.

Following the sale, he was vacationing in Europe. There he saw many Europeans purchasing toothpaste in a pump-style package. He obtained the rights to this type of packaging for the U.S. and proceeded to market pump toothpaste - only to have the same competitive sequence happen that occurred with Soft Soap. He once again sold off the rights to a larger company and began to look at other opportunities.

He felt that he wanted to find something with higher margins and more insulation from large brand manufacturers. He chose perfume and proceeded to find a fragrance that he felt was unique and different enough to garner attention. He only needed to find a name to endorse and help him market it. He decided on Calvin Klein.

As he tells the story, he went to the New York offices and spent several days waiting for the chance to deliver his pitch. At last, the opportunity came and Klein liked the scent and chose the name. But there was one significant hurdle – a huge advertising budget was needed to successfully introduce a new fragrance. Klein agreed to lend his name for a percentage of the retail sales and also would design the advertising.

However my friend had to finance the cost of the advertising...$18 million was the number needed! This was a defining moment. His choice was to "bet the farm" or walk away. To raise that amount of money, it would absolutely take every resource he could tap. It would mean leveraging himself personally, along with his company, to the extent that both would be wiped out if it failed. He chose to go forward and the perfume was launched in November for the Christmas season. It was one of the most successful perfume launches ever! His company not only was saved but the success allowed him to go on and sell the company later and retire in comfort. By the way, the name of the perfume was Obsession.

My own "bet the farm" story comes from my early career in the retail food business. In 1978, I had four retail supermarkets in Rochester, Minnesota. On July 5 of that year, a 100-year flood devastated the city. I had three stores impacted, one of which was totally destroyed. I carried only a $10,000 flood policy. I had $1.5 million in uninsured losses.

I had just finished a major remodel of one of our stores, which managed to max out our lines of credit. In meeting with our attorney, we discussed the possibility of filing for bankruptcy. My banker said that they would extend additional credit to get us back in business but at a high cost. We would be taking on more debt than we ever had in our history. It also meant that since we lost one store completely, we would have to sustain the debt with about a 25 percent reduction in sales.

I also was keenly aware that the public was suspicious of flooded stores, questioning the merchandise. This suspicion was present in spite of the fact that it had been well publicized that the Federal Department of Agriculture had supervised all cleanup.

Faced with all these difficulties, the decision was not easy. But, after meeting with key employees, discussing the situation and the upcoming sacrifices that would have to be made, we did decide to "bet the farm" and go on.

Before it was over, however, I had one more "bet the farm" opportunity.

Prior to the flood, our bank lending agreement had a floating adjustable interest rate and since they also put a floor under the rate, I insisted on a cap. Even though protective floors were common, banks were not accustomed to granting a ceiling. After much haggling, the bank agreed. The interest rate was set at 8.5, the floor at 7.5, and the ceiling at 13 percent. Even though they agreed, my bankers said there was no reason for a ceiling because the chance of interest going that high over the length of the loan was very slim.

After the flood, our financial situation was extremely tight. In order to squeeze the cash flow to pay our debt, the entire management team had bonuses suspended and everyone agreed to no raises until we had paid off the debt. By 1980 interest started to climb and so did the interest on our note. I was comforted by the fact that we had that ceiling. It wasn't long before the bank sent notice that they were going to raise rates well above the 13 percent limit. In fact, in a very short period of time they were at 23 percent!

Our backs were against the wall. The bank had a new president who claimed that our flood borrowing had negated the prior agreement; in effect, we had no agreement and he could charge whatever he wished.

This cash flow nearly caused cardiac arrest. Suddenly, I no longer could pay all our creditors and very soon after that I was faced with meeting our bi-weekly payroll with absolutely no cash whatsoever.

I met with the banker and appealed our case. I was told that my only choice was to file for bankruptcy. I reminded him that we had never signed a new loan agreement so that, as far as I was concerned, the old one held precedence. He told me to sue him.

My next stop was my attorney and he agreed that we had a strong case and he would pursue it. The problem was that I needed cash in two days! So after discussing the situation with our key managers, all of whom said they would forego their wages for the time being, I knew that I had no choice but to find a way through this and go forward without bankruptcy.

I went to a competing bank and met with the president. I told him our situation, of which he was already well aware, and explained that I needed $56,000 to meet my payroll or I essentially, was out of business. I also told him that I had no collateral and explained the size of the debt and the current interest I was being charged. I said all I had was my signature and perhaps my first born, although I wasn't sure at that point whether or not the first bank had claim to him also. With no hesitation, he gave me the money.

Shortly after that, the original bank, after realizing that we would sue on the loan agreement matter, agreed to roll our interest rate back to 13 percent and reimburse us for the higher rate overcharges. We had turned the corner and, within a year, had paid down the first bank far enough to enable us to move the balance of our debt - - and all of our accounts - to the bank that had rescued us.

Defining moments like this will occur for all entrepreneurs at some point in their career. The situations that cause sleepless nights and require the risk of everything, once again, are the things that prevent many from attempting the leap into entrepreneurship in the first place. The "bet the farm" situation does not always allow one to allay risk and limit the downside. These times will test one's self, belief system, team and belief in an Almighty Being. Ralph Waldo Emerson once said, "It was a high counsel that I once heard given to a young person, 'Always do what you are afraid to do.'"

"Who bravely dares must sometimes risk a fall"
                                    -Tobias George Smollett

Section Two: Initiation to Birth

"Make the most of yourself,
for that is all there is!"
Ralph Waldo Emerson

Chapter Two

"All I Need is an Idea, Right?"
(What more is there to do?)

There is a phenomenon, which for lack of a better term, I will call "inventor's syndrome."

It occurs most often in inventors who may or may not be entrepreneurs. It is readily identified in a person who fails to see the full value created by an entrepreneurial event. The person afflicted with inventor's syndrome believes all or most of the value exists in the idea. There is little understanding of the capital, research, time and organizational talent it will take to realize full success.

Ideas alone very rarely contain much value. The idea itself may be only worth about 10 percent of the initial value of the opportunity.

People with the "inventor's syndrome" are best described by a Ralph Waldo Emerson quote, "Build a better mousetrap and the world will beat a path to your door."

Now consider this: The mousetrap is the most invented machine in American history. There are over 4,400 patents, with 40 new ones issued every year. Four hundred patents are turned down each year. Only 24 mousetrap patent holders have made money from their patent. The most successful patent was issued in 1903 to John Mast under the trade name "Victor." Manufactured by the Woodstream Corporation, Victor's annual sales are $30 million, greater than all the other mousetraps combined. The Victor's spring-loaded trap with its familiar wooden base has maintained its large market share through fully automated assembly and low cost.

Scar Tissue Event One: Misunderstood Value

"With this idea I can simply retire, right?"

Many first-time entrepreneurs feel that the idea is the all-encompassing point of entrepreneurial development. The first step, then, is to go and find the money. Reality hits with growing awareness that the idea is worth little or nothing. Unfortunately, reality can be slow to arrive. I have known inventors who spent years pursuing money for an idea that is no longer viable.

A few years ago, Pepper...and Salt, the daily Wall Street Journal cartoon, illustrated misunderstood value. The cartoon showed two young entrepreneurs talking with a potential financial backer and the caption was, "We've invested our hearts and souls in this company. We're only asking you to invest 10 million."

Inventors and entrepreneurs are quite often two separate people. A common sequence of events happens when an entrepreneur recognizes the value of an inventor's idea and secures the right to commercially pursue or produce the opportunity.

This Idea is Worth Millions

One day in my office at the University of St. Thomas I was visited by a would-be entrepreneur. I'll call him Fred. He had recently obtained the rights to a wound-healing device from the University of Minnesota. The device used miniscule direct current directly applied to the skin around a wound to speed healing. Everyone who witnessed the first use of the technology was excited. Everyone, that is, except for many in the medical community, who had trouble accepting the basic concept.

Fred felt people should be lined up to invest. He asked me to help him raise money and we developed a private placement memorandum. In this process we began to assess how much money was needed and how much equity he was willing to give up. Fred felt he had a world-beater piece of technology; all he had to do was borrow a little more money to finance the company through the Food and Drug Administration approval process.

When finally convinced that with no sales and no cash flow the company could not possibly handle debt, he resigned to an equity sale, proposing he give up 5 to 10 percent of the company to raise $1 million. His proposal suggested that this "idea" was worth $10 million. Fred, as incredible as it may seem, had no trouble suggesting that maybe $10 million was not high enough.

I went on to explain to him that it was not unusual in the type of company he was attempting to start, to have equity cut in half with each round of investment. I told him that if he were successful, he would be lucky to own 1 to 5 percent of the company at the end. He was not pleased.

Since Fred still did not have a full complement of scar tissue, we went ahead as he demanded and held an investor meeting. Not surprisingly, no one invested. A quick meeting with Fred and the accounting firm resulted in a redo of the investment memorandum. This time he reluctantly offered 40 percent of the company for $500,000. The money was raised in one investor meeting.

Fred's next round of scar tissue soon followed.

Prototype development and FDA-required clinical trials ate up the $500,000 in a year. More investment was needed. I suggested he give up another 50 percent of his company's equity, leaving him with 30 percent. The message of the need for more capital was delivered at multiple board meetings (I had agreed to sit on the board earlier). At each meeting he said no, while the cash was rapidly disappearing.

It was not long before the money was completely gone. Fred resigned as company CEO at the last board meeting, refusing to acknowledge that his own unwillingness to give up equity had resulted in the company's demise.

As Paul Harvey would say, "Now for the rest of the story."

As Fred withdrew from the company, he shut the door on contact with me as well as his stockholders.

Through a sense of obligation to the stockholders, I found a small medical device company that was looking for new product ideas. Through contact with Fred's attorney. I inquired what it would take for him to sell his 60 percent equity stake. He responded that it would take $10 million. After extended negotiations, he accepted $250,000. I then proposed a deal where the acquiring company would purchase the 60 percent share for cash and then exchange their stock (at the same valuation) from the balance of the shareholders. Since they were a public company there was an established value for the stock.

On the day we were to close on the deal, I received a phone call from the CEO of the acquiring company. He apologized - the deal was off - his company had just been acquired by a larger one. I was devastated and at a loss about what to do next.

That afternoon I was coming from a meeting at a large public accounting office when I ran into the individual that had introduced me to the potential buyer. He started to congratulate me, knowing the deal should have closed. When I told him what happened he said, "Good, I was hoping for that as I have found financial backers and would like to buy it for myself."

Luck occurs in strange ways! We sold the company on the originally negotiated terms. This individual also purchased other medical technology with existing sales to provide cash flow for the further development of the wound care device. The additional technology started to grow and eventually became Advanced Respiratory. The product was a vest-like device that was attached to an air compressor. It would inflate and squeeze the chest of children and adults afflicted with cystic fibrosis to relieve them of accumulated phlegm. In about 10 years, the company sold. The original investors received nearly a ten-fold return on their initial investment.

A Different School of Thought on Idea Value

Keith Thorndyke, a former graduate student of mine looked at funding his opportunity with a different perspective. First, he spent time researching the need (soon to become a requirement through a new state law) to recycle fluorescent bulbs to remove their mercury content and keep that out of landfills. He then discovered technology in Sweden that would allow him to do that very thing.

He went about recruiting fellow students as team members. Each had unique skills that could help move the idea along. The group met weekly to plan.

Thorndyke estimated that the high cost of the equipment ($880,000), the installation, and finally financing the gap until sales began would necessitate raising as much as $1 million. The equipment was a primary concern. The Swedish company required $288,000 be paid down when the equipment was loaded, followed by $72,000 at the U.S. port and another $72,000 upon acceptance. He was able to negotiate with the Swedish company to take back a note for $160,000 of the total price, reducing his up-front needs to $720,000.

He recognized that he would need to raise this amount of money privately and, if successful, he might be able to raise the balance in bank debt. In conferring with his advisers, he decided to offer 50 percent of the company for the $400,000. He immediately went about getting his private placement memorandum finished and began to contact potential investors. He needed to act fast; competitors were entering the market as awareness of the new legislation developed.

As of the date he had set to confirm the order and pay the $288,000, he had raised only $300,000. Following a hurried meeting of his advisers, he decided to go ahead and confirm the order and immediately go back to the original group of investors and ask them to double down on their investment. The strategy worked. Recyclights went on to be a successful company, which was sold five years after its founding.

These are two distinctly different entrepreneurial stories. In one, the entrepreneur was overly enamored with the value of the idea and allowed greed to enter into the picture. His unwillingness to share enough equity to raise the amount of capital needed assured that the initial business would fail. In the second example, the entrepreneur's focus on doing whatever it took assured eventual success. Both entrepreneurs earned some scar tissue along the way. Thorndyke's scar tissue was more of the Band-Aid variety while Fred's was a fatal incision.

The initial idea is just a very small part of the infinite array of details that go into creating value in an entrepreneurial event. Fred attempted to leap from idea to money while Thorndyke took the time to refine the concept by assembling a competent team, developing a successful plan, and raising the right amount of money.

The Process of Success Development

Rajiv Tandon taught for me at the University of St. Thomas. He developed a chart of what he called the "Process of Success Development." This chart did not follow from scientific research, but rather came from several faculty sitting around and estimating the probability scale based upon their own personal experience.

Money most generally will follow opportunity, not the other way around. Securing funding for an idea only enhances the chance of success to 25 percent. Developing and growing sales will increase the odds of success to about 60 percent. Sustaining the needed management and sales support will take the organization the rest of the way.

Process of Success Development

Step One
Probability
Person with idea...1%

Step Two
Opportunity..5%
Hurdle: Attracting Talent

Step Three
Founding Team..10%

Step Four
Venture Plans...15%
Hurdle: Flawed Planning

Step Five
Achieving Funding..25%
Hurdle: Initial Sales

Step Six
Beginning Sales...40%

Step Seven
Sales Growth..60%
Hurdle "Transition"

Step Eight
Initial Success

This chart gives another perspective on the role of value within the entrepreneurial enterprise.

The value steps related to exhibiting a viable opportunity consists of:

· Exhibiting a true understanding of the marketplace. Knowing the major competitors, understanding the factors that will allow competition in this segment, having a grasp of the timing and the conditions necessary for all of this to happen.

· Understanding quite precisely the amount of capital necessary and how it will be deployed.

· Having a competent and committed team.

· Having a descriptive plan, a developed and tested product/service, and well identified customers.

It is imperative that at least this much accomplished to find support for an entrepreneurial venture.

Scar Tissue Event Two: Control vs. Upside Potential

"I would prefer to own 100 percent of something small!"

While moving through the steps of successful development, it will soon become apparent if resources beyond the entrepreneur's are needed.

If the potential creation has greater needs, the entrepreneur will need to engage in a little self-reflection about what's at stake. If the opportunity has very large potential, it must be allowed to grow beyond the limits of personal control. This is the next potential pitfall and potential for additional scar tissue.

If the entrepreneur cannot become comfortable with the thought of some day turning over control of this entity to someone else, then he/she should not pursue an endeavor that could have substantial scale potential.

For many entrepreneurs, the primary objective is to grow the idea as large as possible...meaning the venture may achieve mass that is well beyond the limits of their personal control. For others the mere thought of someone else gaining control of their "baby" can cause them to become physically ill. One needs to decide early on which type of person he/she might be and then be sure to identify the type of opportunity that will fit those desires.

A momentary glance again at the "Process of Success Development Chart" illustrates that once opportunity is defined and well articulated, there is another hurdle or potential for additional scar tissue.

Scar Tissue Event Three: Team vs. solo event

"After all it is my Idea."

Successful ventures are created from teams of people with complementary skills. It does not take long to recognize that it is a rare person skilled in the vast array of things needed for a successful venture.

The entrepreneur must spend time carefully selecting team members, as well as determining the number needed. Team members should counterbalance the entrepreneur's weaknesses and demonstrate similar commitment to making the venture a reality. All too often an entrepreneurial leader will take more time selecting a tie to wear than a potential future partner.

One of my students started a venture while in graduate school. He experienced initial success but desperately needed assistance in the venture. He chose his high school friend and roommate. To entice the friend, "Cliff" gave him 25 percent of the company. The friend was not college-educated and had no managerial experience.

I questioned the skills this friend brought to the table, but Cliff was not concerned - he just needed some "physical help." I then questioned the wisdom of giving away a big chunk of equity at this early date. Cliff replied that he thought it was a fair thing to do for a friend; the company was not worth that much anyway. A major scar tissue event had its beginnings in that comment.

Three years later Cliff came to my office to complain about his partner. The company had experienced a great deal of success and had outgrown the skills that his buddy had brought to the table. Consequently this person was now just taking up space and not contributing. Cliff wanted him out.

I explained that this was going to be much more difficult now that he had given him 25 percent of the company. The friend had hired an attorney and was seeking a large settlement. Cliff asked me if I would help negotiate it and I agreed. The settlement figure we reached was $250,000.

Cliff ranted and raved about the lack of contribution and questioned why he should agree to pay this individual so much money at a time when, with the growth of the company, he could put that money to much better use. I encouraged him to take the deal and he eventually did. I told Cliff he would look back on the settlement as a very cheap solution to heal the wound.

When Cliff sold his company about seven years later for $40 million, I called him and reminded him of my advice. He admitted I had been right about the buyout price. He also said that he wished he had listened to me about taking the time to select the right partner in the beginning.

Finding and selecting a partner is not an easy task. Examine which skills are critical for the business to be successful. One does not need an equity partner for easily employable skills. An open discussion of values, both personal and business, is also critical. Mismatched values are almost always impossible to resolve. Values are entrenched in the human psyche when we are very young. They are very hard, if not impossible, to change. When values between two people in a working relationship do not match, the relationship will come apart.

Billionaire entrepreneur and founder of University Computing, Sam Wyly, was asked in a September 1, 2008 interview with Forbes.com what he looked for in a manager. He responded that he particularly looked for someone who exhibited a history of getting things done through other people and someone who had high personal integrity.

Melanie Lindner, also wrote on the topic on April 28, 2008 on Forbes.com. Her work, titled, What to Look for in a Business Partner, identified key characteristics/issues:

· A person who can compromise without being too compromising

· Solid contacts that are important to help the venture

· Responsible people who do not carry any personal baggage especially large unpaid bills

· Early agreement on who is in charge and how critical decisions will be made

· Early agreement on compensation, how, when and how much

Another key issue to consider is equity sharing. If the selected partner is making a personal investment in cash, intellectual property or donated time (or all of the above) the entrepreneur must assess the value of each and determine how much equity he/she is willing to give up to acquire that expertise. Remembering, all the while, that if this new partner is a friend, the business relationship may work differently than a personal one.

David Gage who authored, The Partnership Charter, (Basic Press, 2004) suggests personality tests to fully understand everyone's strengths and weaknesses. He suggests each partner write down expectations for the entity being created. Issues covered should include: profits and equity to be shared; who will be responsible for what and how decisions will be made. It would also be good to discuss a variety of hypothetical situations around ethics, leave time, health issues, etc. This assessment should take place during a two, or three, day retreat.

After expectations have been written, documents need to be shared and compared. Then one comprehensive document should be written and placed within the final legal partnership agreement. Once this is completed, partners may wish to more formally discuss ownership arrangements or equity sharing. Equity is a precious commodity. Even though in the beginning it may seem valueless, as in Cliff's case, it is where the real money is to be made.

Other Partnership Issues

Never (NOT EVER) agree to a 50/50 ownership arrangement. For every one successful, I can give two examples of such partnerships that did not make it. I have known of partnerships, which have lasted 25 years and then one day there is disagreement. With a 50/50 arrangement, nothing is resolved and the business decision is stymied. In most cases, it is the beginning of the end for the partnership. One person must have majority control and that decision should be up-front and immediate.

I know of only one 50/50 business relationship that worked. It was a business founded by two women who knew in advance the pitfalls of this type of partnership. They worked out a prior agreement to visit a marriage counselor whenever one or the other felt the need to better define their relationship. They chose to work out differences through a marriage counselor because this was a professional trained to work with 50/50 relationships.

Once the ownership split has been agreed upon, a partnership agreement is next. This is no time for handshake agreements. Everything must be in writing. Whatever legal costs are incurred, it will seem cheap in the end. An effective partnership agreement should include addressing questions such as: Who has authority to borrow money? How will profits be split? What will wages be? How will wage increases be determined? When will wage increases be considered? How might a partner get out of the venture? What happens in the case of debilitating illness? What happens if one partner dies? And, in the case that partners can no longer work together – who will buy the other out and how?

Partners must have a buy-sell agreement, which spells out specifics. Valuation (a fair industry standard) of the business is critical as is how valuation is determined. I recommend hiring an outside firm to keep it equitable. An arbitration clause to avoid any unnecessary attorney fees also is desirable. Anything not discussed or left to chance can and will resurface in the case of disagreement. Even the importance of carrying life insurance on each partner in order to prevent a crippling loss should be on the table as agreement terms are decided.

Partnerships are not easy. But when they do come together in the right way they go a long way toward helping the entrepreneur cope with the stress of owning a business by sharing heavy responsibilities.

Remember that compatibility is driven by a set of commonly held values that will further create a lasting successful business relationship. I previously warned of the dangers of sharing too much equity too soon. On the other hand, not sharing any equity can send a message of greed and make it difficult to find and retain great talent that can help the venture achieve true success. Equity inspires and attracts people to an entrepreneurial event.

Of course, finding an equity partner is only the tip of the iceberg in building a well-rounded team. I firmly believe that the process of finding team members should start with identifying one or more senior mentors to help guide through the process and avoid serious mistakes that could lead to an early acquisition of scar tissue.

Scar Tissue Event Four: Failure to Broadly Seek out Advice

"Secrecy is the best policy, isn't it?"

Much like "Pre-Scar Tissue Event" that I described previously, this one occurs after an entrepreneur has refined the idea and begun the start-up process. There is now fear that with launch so close and all of the unique ideas that have added value, sharing is too great a risk.

This causes many to attempt to veil their idea in secrecy - not telling anyone but a few key people directly involved. At this juncture, secrecy can be a fatal mistake.

In the first pre-scar tissue event, it was only an idea or rough concept that required feedback. Now, feedback on the execution will ensure that all bases are covered. The entrepreneur needs feedback about everything from production sourcing, to order fulfillment, to target marketing. The input net must be cast wider.

In most societies, the wisdom of experience is greatly admired and sought out. In the U.S., in the early days of Silicon Valley and again with the

Internet phenomenon, many were caught up in the excitement of youthful ideas.

Youthful entrepreneurs in those days often carried an air of arrogance coupled with an uncanny ability to make much money - fast. Some were unwilling to embrace the leavening effect of experienced entrepreneurs. I remember being at an entrepreneurial conference in California when a young man, who seemed to be about 18 years old, came up to me and asked what I did. When I explained that I had left my business career to create a collegiate program to teach entrepreneurs, he looked at me incredulously and responded that he did not understand why would anyone bother to take the time to study this topic when all you had to do was come up with an idea and people would throw money at you.

Sadly, his commentary was serious. He claimed to be a multi-millionaire and wondered if I knew so much, why wasn't I out there making millions like he was? The subsequent disastrous failures of many young people like him with a lack of respect for the wisdom of experienced entrepreneurs and callous disregard for essential management principles speak volumes.

Identifying Mentors

Building an advisory team from the beginning

will go a long way to helping make an idea both enjoyable and successful. The entrepreneur should seek out at least two or three people who are willing to be brutally honest and totally objective. Senior people with relevant industry experience to advise and serve as mentors are preferable. Better still is someone who has had start-up experience either as an investor or as an entrepreneur. The entrepreneur should not plan on mentors becoming investors and that should be clarified up front.

Mentors should be given specific information about what is needed from them. They should be assured that they will not be inundated with materials or assignments and their time will not be abused. Initial meetings can be scheduled monthly, then quarterly later. Meetings with each mentor should be no more than an hour at an early breakfast. (The entrepreneur always picks up the tab.) Meetings are best when they are pre-planned, with a concise and specific agenda.

The search to identify potential mentors needs to begin with an honest assessment of self and knowledge gaps. Referrals from those who may have specific "chunks of knowledge" can assist in the process.

This process will help identify more permanent mentor relationships with experienced persons who may be willing to serve on a long-term basis. Do not ask mentors to serve on a board of directors - most have more opportunities than they can count. A mentor is more like a guidepost, serving as a periodic checkpoint.

A mentor of mine helped me see a multi-million dollar opportunity that I likely would never have sought out. I grew up in the retail food industry and spent the bulk of my business life in the field. Back in the 70's the retail food industry was experiencing lack-luster growth in spite of population increases.

It took little study to discover the fast food industry was experiencing growth rates five to 10 times as great as the retail grocery industry. Obviously, they were cutting into our business. We soon embarked on the development of in-store bakeries, deli departments and other ventures that helped us focus on the convenience take-out market.

These measures helped but did not stem the growth of fast food. At the time, my mentor, who was not part of the food industry, asked me a key question: "Since this indirect competitive onslaught seems unstoppable wouldn't it be easier to join them than fight them?" I had never before considered that alternative. The result was that I was able to put together an investment group that ended up building a successful fast food company that, at one time, totaled 13 restaurants. When we sold the bulk of this company, the proceeds were greater than from the sale of my retail food stores. This was an opportunity that would have been totally missed were it not for one question from a friend and mentor.

In addition to face-to-face mentors, there are Internet sources that are very helpful. One was started by Forbes online magazine: http://smallbizexchange. forbes.com/. This site requires one to join but there is no cost. The site features experts, entrepreneurs and company contacts. In addition there is a section called "Ask An Expert," containing contact information for experts in various disciplines who are available to answer questions.

Other Internet Sources

· www.micromentor.org - A nonprofit which helps identify mentors online by offering profiles and contact information.

· www.imantri.com - A social networking site for entrepreneurs, which also can help identify online mentoring contacts.

· www.gobignetwork.com - Another site with help for financing along with mentoring information.

· www.jumpstart.com - A site with a page called, IdeaCrossing, which helps discover potential mentors.

All of these resources can help save time and develop an efficient list of online contacts. As with any online contacts, screen carefully and exercise caution with information shared. My suggestion: Utilize these sources as backup for the personal face-to-face mentors developed locally.

Professional advisors, specifically an attorney and an accountant, must be selected immediately following the selection of mentors. I would always select people who are familiar with the entrepreneurial process and have a reputation for helping fledging entrepreneurs become successful. At this point, the venture and its entrepreneur may have little or no credibility. Choosing wisely here will increase credibility in the local community.

A network of mentors can serve as a referral source, helping plug identified holes where specialized critical skills are necessary for total success. Take time to vet these carefully. Check backgrounds and verify track records before meeting with potential mentors or advisors. As in the scar tissue story cited previously, the best tavern-hopping friend does not make the cut.

Scar Tissue Event Five: Failing to Write a Plan

"Everyone knows what to do, we can muck through this!"

Looking further at the "Process of Success Development," note the plan is next in order. Needless to say it is the "game plan" for the new venture. If done right it should last at least through the funding process. "Did I read that right?" one might ask. Planning is a never ending task and many things will change, the amount and type of money raised, the reality of the market, geographical issues, and so on. A plan needs to be flexible.

Is it needed? I would say yes, only from the perspective that it helps everyone involved with the company know and understand the overall vision and what needs to be done first. I liken the business plan to a roadmap that can illustrate to both entrepreneur and employee the critical path that must be followed to achieve ultimate objectives.

A plan will save time and show correct choices when decisions are difficult. It will also provide milestones to measure success. Are there people who start businesses without one? Definitely yes, myself being one. But without one, the entrepreneur will find that the 24/7 demands in the beginning will be intensified tremendously.

If the business team has participated in the development of the plan, they will know it intimately and instinctively know how to react to many of the situations that will arise. It needs to be concisely written (no more than 20-25 pages!) and focused on all the critical pieces and steps that are needed to make the venture a success. I will not go into detail here about the construction of the plan - there are many books and software that do an adequate job. (Two popular software programs are: BizPlan Builder: www.jian.com and BusinessPlanPro: www.palo-alto.com.) However, I will say that a "Unique Selling Proposition" should be included in the plan. This proposition identifies why someone should purchase the venture's product or service.

I have most likely read at least 2,000 business plans and written about 20 or so of my own. However, this does not make me an expert on design, layout or formatting. Each plan is unique and must reflect a dream as the entrepreneur sees it. A business plan written by a consultant will perhaps stand out, but I can almost guarantee that the investment community will reject it out of hand.

What will an investor look for? I can speak only from my own experience, but I believe a plan must include five interdependent components.

The Five Interdependent Components

- The customer

- The team

- The opportunity

- The environment

- Critical risks and rewards.

The Customer

- Clearly articulate who the customer will be. How many of these potential customers have been spoken to and what's their interest level? Why do these people wish to buy this product or service? How will these people be reached? And, will this be easy or difficult?

The Team

- Explain thoroughly just who is involved. How many people are associated with this venture, both inside and outside? Where are they from? What is their relevant experience and what qualifies them to be part of this venture? Have they worked together before? How did they come together? Do their skills fit the opportunity and are these skills complementary? What are their collective past accomplishments? What is the educational preparation of each team member? What is their reputation in the business community? Is the team realistic about any gaps in skills that may exist? How will the venture continue to attract and keep high quality people? Has the team had experience with adversity in making hard choices and decisions? What is the exhibited commitment to this venture? What are their values and motivations? Is there a complete understanding of both the upside and downside of the particular venture?

The Opportunity

· Crisply articulate the opportunity itself. Is the market well understood in terms of size, growth rate, and the length of time it will exist? How will the product/service be priced? (Too often new entrepreneurs assume that the best pricing strategy is to be the cheapest in the market place. The problem with this assumption is that with any growth at all they soon will be faced with many additional costs without the margin to pay for them. Personally, I would rather see projections based on a strong value-added approach with above average margins justified with additional features and superb service.) How well does the company understand its customer and the competition? How will a purchase decision be made and how long might it take? Are there compelling reasons for a customer to make this buy? What will it cost for the company to acquire, maintain and retain its customers? Is the distribution network well laid out and fully understood? Of course this all needs to be neatly summed up in an attached financial plan with spreadsheets and at least three years of performance estimated.

The Environment

· Explain the environment the business is entering. Are there supporting conditions that will help drive product/service sales? It is easier to grow a business when customer needs help dictate the purchase rather than having to be "missionary salespeople." Are there any regulatory or other governmental issues that can impact development in any way? Finally, does the entrepreneur really understand who the customer is? I cannot begin to count the number of blank stares I have received from entrepreneurs, whose business plans I have reviewed, when I ask them, "Assuming that I fund you today, who is the first customer you will call?"

Critical Risks and Rewards

· Identify all the risks associated with the venture. Has everything possible been done to reduce these to an absolute minimum? Are contingency plans in place when things do not go as planned? Is there an exhibited understanding of the need for investor rewards? What are the identified ways this might happen? Have various possible exit strategies been explored?

Finally, I like to see a vision statement. It should consist of three parts: mission, purpose and values. There should be no misunderstanding of what the team wishes to accomplish and how it will be accomplished. The mission gives people something to work toward; the purpose provides something around which to rally; values guide how it will be done.

It could be argued that for the entrepreneur not seeking outside capital this type of painful research and plan development is unnecessary – a waste of valuable time. I can name many who have just forged ahead. I also can name many who have lost an entire life savings because they failed to spend this planning time up front. Why not fail on paper before jumping in and failing with real money?

Chapter Three

"As you take the plunge into life's ocean, remember to make some waves!"
Daryl Erdman

**"What an Idea; Now All I Need is Money!
(or 'The Great Leap')"**

Very few successful entrepreneurial events can occur without some form of capital infusion. It is nice if the entrepreneur has enough personal net worth to be able to launch the venture without any outside financial assistance. However, that does not happen very often. An opportunity worth pursuing will generally require resources beyond those under personal control.

Quite often, after spending months researching an opportunity, finding interested team members and writing a business plan all that remains is that last critical piece - money. The entrepreneur will believe it is such an obvious opportunity that people will be eager to help launch the venture financially. Timing is critical and a large chunk of capital has already been spent getting to this point. Anxiety begins to set in with objections and turndowns. For the entrepreneur, it is hard to understand why potential investors cannot see this wonderful opportunity.

If the right, targeted investors are given the opportunity to invest, the "yes" will usually come quickly. It is the "no" that is protracted. Why is that? I believe that it is generally difficult for people to turn someone down. It is much easier to just put the decision off. When this occurs, it is always best to move on quickly. Those who claim they need more time or assurances will, most likely, eventually decline. Investors who genuinely like the concept will come to an investment decision early.

The process of finding investors can be enhanced substantially with a solid funding proposal. Take time to assess the relevant experience of the team and plug any evident holes. Limiting the downside risk through careful structuring can further enhance the proposal. Investment can be staged in several tranches with milestone requirements. Demonstrating how some investment might be recovered in case of total failure is helpful. Conversely, exhibit the total amount of the upside potential related to the amount of investment. It also helps to discuss how this upside will eventually be realized and in what time frame. Exhibiting ways and means to shorten the time to positive cash flow and eventual profitability are positives. The team's commitment through willingness to sacrifice salary to assure success also should be noted.

Scar Tissue Event Six

Funding (any money will do)

Finding the right source and getting that source to invest is very time consuming. This process is complicated by the fact that many entrepreneurs fail to spend the time to determine the type of investment that will best fit their opportunity. The knee jerk reaction is to start knocking on doors rather than spending upfront time analyzing the type of investment that would work best and then qualifying those in the investment community who might have an interest. Too many potentially great ideas end unfunded, not because the idea was bad, but because the entrepreneur sought money in all the wrong places.

Looking for what many call "dumb" money, or money that people will just hand over based on a promise to do good, is not a sound financing approach. Better money generally is the more difficult to obtain. I say this because that is usually money (whether debt or equity) that will come from professional sources that will ask really hard questions that, in the end, will help develop a better venture. Therefore, right sourcing a venture fund is critical.

The first decision, besides the amount of money needed, is the type of money best suited to the venture – debt or equity. Financing with debt may be attractive, but holds the potential for disaster. The ability to do so hinges on two key factors: 1) If financing with debt, it is essential that cash flow start immediately. Immediate cash flow usually involves some form of retail event, when a product source is already lined up with willing customers. 2) The financial plan must include the cost of servicing the debt. Margins must cover the initial business expenses plus debt service.

The amount of money needed can be determined through developing a projected cash flow financial statement. As a rule-of-thumb, nearly double an initial projection is the right amount. Achieving sales projections generally takes two to three times longer than initially estimated. Countless minute details cost time in the beginning. Some examples of early time consuming activities include getting computers hooked up and programmed, getting telephones activated and even finding office space.

Bootstrapping – An Alternative to Debt

"Bootstrapping," or launching a venture without seeking any outside capital, can be a difficult feat, but if successful the entrepreneur owns all equity. Nearly immediate cash flow is essential as is looking down every possible avenue to conserve cash. Bootstrapping requires a great deal of creativity and some extremely hard work, but is very rewarding and self-fulfilling for those who succeed. Listed below, suggested tactics for those considering debt-free financing.

Bootstrap Funding Tactics

Avoid buying anything new. Borrow, rent or lease.

This means finding space that may not cost to rent (a basement, a converted bedroom or a garage will do nicely). The same holds true for equipment. I knew one entrepreneur who used public library computers to avoid buying extra ones. Universities and major companies many times have used desks and chairs that can be purchased quite reasonably. Shop garage sales for lamps and other furniture. Sell a new car and replace it with a good used one.

Leverage everything possible.

A friend of mine started an electronic controls company. He had many ideas to improve upon a wide range of industrial controls. Although not an engineer himself, he made deals with friends who had design credentials to develop these products in exchange for a "royalty" which, in this case, was a percentage of sales. Today he has a multi-faceted company with his own engineering team and sales of more than $50 million. Find creative ways to limit early cash outlay. Do everything possible to keep overhead low.

Find the cheapest possible space.

If outside space is necessary, a landlord could fund leasehold improvements and spread payments over the length of the lease. Contrary to popular thought, a prestigious address generally will not impress potential investors. Meet customers in public places if traveling to them is not possible. One entrepreneur used the local airport to give the impression that he was busy developing markets through extensive travel. I have known others who convinced their attorney or accountant to use one of their meeting rooms. Another solid tactic is to meet for breakfast. Early meetings convey that one is too busy during regular office hours (often true). If this is a customer, the entrepreneur must pick up the tab and breakfast is by far the cheapest meal of the day.

Draw minimal salary and use credit card debt sparingly.

The first is most important - it shows both commitment and confidence. If necessary, one can trade equity to substitute for salary. The use of credit debt is a decision that must be weighed. Any early stage debt can strangle. It is an obligation that not only will require monthly payments but also carries a high interest cost. That said, I have known many who have used this method to carry them to positive cash flow. Much depends on the type of business and how quickly cash flow can be achieved. Some ventures, such as retail, will be able to generate cash almost immediately. Others that require much research and development can lengthen the timeline to sales by years.

Look for ways to create "tradeouts."

Marketable skills can be traded rather than purchased. For example, I know a young woman who started a Yoga studio. She traded lessons for web site design, marketing expertise and even outside accounting. I also know of a software company where engineers would contract consulting services to supplement income. Barter can be a very effective cash conservation method.

Negotiate terms on everything!

Try to obtain extended credit terms from key suppliers, advance payments from key customers and barter products/services for outside products/ services.

Conserve cash every way possible!

Control receivables, get advanced payments, give incentives for cash or early pay and apply rigorous credit checks. Monitor accounts receivable like a hawk. Stretch payables by negotiating extended credit terms. Use a monthly cash flow statement with six to 12 month rolling projections.

Marketing and Sales

Look for unused advertising space and negotiate - a trade-out is preferable. Manage inventories to be as close to "just-in-time" as possible. Look to strategic alliances to assist in marketing/distribution. Participate in all related trade shows and volunteer to put on educational seminars related to the industry. Look for cross-promotional opportunities.

People resources

If available, use college interns and moonlighting professionals. Look for competent retired people and use part-time flexible scheduling. Develop and execute training from within.

Frugality Pays – Two Examples

In 2007, I had the privilege of attending the opening of a new facility for a business that was started by one of my students while he was enrolled in St. Thomas graduate program.

Steve Schmidt recognized that at the time he was looking for his opportunity, a new technology with very broad application capability was coming on the scene. That technology was bar code labeling. Schmidt pursued this technology finding industry niches where few were applying it and grew his business from a spare bedroom in his home. Fifteen years have past and now AbeTech is in new facilities in Rogers, Minnesota and enjoying sales of well into eight figures.

He accomplished all this utilizing his own resources and now has full service capabilities in integrated bar coding, RFID (radio frequency identification) labeling, mobile computing and labeling solutions. He has seven offices in five other states and has a wonderful record of growth. I wrote in his final business plan that the opportunity seemed to be large enough to seek outside funding in order to grow faster. Did he make a mistake by not taking this advice? I doubt it. He might have experienced faster sales growth but he also would not have been able to enjoy the feeling of independence and success he gained from going it alone.

Another student picked a far different field to enter. As an undergraduate, Nikki Robbins spent numerous hours in my office expressing her dream of entering the childcare field. The problem was that Robbins had no money, but her desire and willingness to work hard toward her goal stood out.

By working with Robbins, we were able to secure financing by having her sell advance discounted fees to families interested in placing their child in her center. She launched Peace of Mind Daycare in Woodbury, Minnesota soon after graduation. She built it into the largest private child daycare center in a single location (over 300 children) in the state. She has since expanded by building a private elementary school, Footprints Academy. Both entities have many unique services that attract parents from great distances. Needless to say, Robbins is still excited by her creation.

Venture Capital – How it Works

When I was teaching, many of my students assumed that venture capital was necessary anytime resources beyond the entrepreneur's means were needed. Many students had heard or read something about venture capital and had gained limited knowledge. Newspaper articles relayed how young companies were venture capital financed and so consequently, this seemed like the logical place to turn for capital.

Most students, however, did not really understand how the industry worked or what was needed in order to receive financing. I still find this lack of understanding to be prevalent today largely because the industry, itself, has done an inadequate job of explaining to the public how it works.

Since I have had the opportunity to work in the industry as a "venture capitalist," I will attempt to clear up some of the mystery behind the profession.

Most business people recognize that a venture company raises money from other individuals and institutions (i.e. pension funds, insurance companies, banks, etc.). In addition, these companies also pool their own capital. The fund is organized as a limited partnership with a 10-year life (most standard form). Each fund is organized uniquely and with its own focus regarding size (amount of money raised) and investment objectives. Funds range in size from a few million dollars to well over a billion.

Venture capital is considered a high-risk form of investment, thus the return objectives are very high. Choosing investments is not a science and bad investment choices will happen in every fund. Consequently, good investments need to overcome those losses in order for the return to the investors to be above average.

Funds over the years have exhibited a wide variety of returns. During the Internet frenzy, there were funds with returns approaching several hundred percent. More realistically, most funds try to return somewhere in the 25 to 35 percent range.

Why should an entrepreneur be concerned about this? This plays a vital role in the pricing decisions (valuation) that a venture capitalist needs to make about the company. Venture capitalists know going into the negotiation that they will need to make a 50 to 60 percent projected annual return in order to overcome losses and net 25 to 35 percent returns. This comes as a shock to many entrepreneurs.

Venture capitalists also need to realize that return in a relatively short time frame.

Remember that the venture capital company will self-destruct, so to speak, in 10 years. Thinking about how and when that will occur is essential for the entrepreneur. Usually, the end comes through some kind of sale or merger. A sale could be to another company or to the public through an initial public offering.

To many, this prospect is unthinkable. The business is the entrepreneur's legacy. There is nothing wrong with holding this perspective, but the would-be entrepreneur must realize that such a philosophy will exempt one from venture-type financing.

There are other factors to consider when approaching a venture-capital company for financing.

Venture capital companies have traditionally been thinly managed, with a small number of partners making investment decisions. Each partner will be required to provide oversight to the companies in which they have investments. That span of control most generally should not exceed 10 companies. For example, a large fund (say $500 million) that has five partners would probably make a total of 50 investments and limit them to $10 million per deal. The entrepreneur must ask what size investment the company is willing to make.

Each fund will have committed investment criteria. The venture-capital company will identify an industry and business development-stage focus.

Industry focus is largely determined by the background and experience of the managing partners. The entrepreneur must pre-determine funds likely to invest in his/her industry segment.

The development-stage focus is somewhat dictated by the experience factor as well as the fund size. A larger fund making larger investments will usually focus on more developed companies because they will generally be able to handle the larger investments required. Very few funds will focus on raw start-up ventures because the risk is too high.

A venture-capital firm looks at four broad risk factors: management (strengths and weaknesses), business concept/technology (whether or not it works and is scalable), market potential (and if market size is proportional to support the company growth projections), and lastly, sales potential (have real customers actually purchased this service/product?). In order for a company to limit this risk assessment they generally will have to prove the concept and have demonstrated real sales.

Ideally, the entrepreneur must be able to show average growth propensity, necessary for an above average return to the venture capitalist. Convertible preferred stock is usually the preferred investment vehicle. It further enhances the venture-capital company return, but will cut into the entrepreneurial company's cash flow.

Lastly, the entrepreneur should assess the reasonableness of the request. A blockbuster idea with proven multi-million dollar sales potential and ready customers will more easily find a multi-million dollar investment than the proposal seeking the same amount of money with an unproven market and more limited demand. Be cognizant of the potential to utilize a very large investment over a reasonable time. It will be difficult to raise several million dollars up front if not all the money will be needed for several years. It may cost less equity to raise money in multiple rounds after milestones have been achieved.

Venture capital is not for everyone. It requires commitment to above average growth, which extends beyond the limits of personal control. The goal must be building value for everyone and not just oneself. The entrepreneur should be more interested in capturing this opportunity than a large ownership percentage. And finally, turning to venture capital demands a willingness to listen to others and commitment to some form of harvest.

Angel Networks

Another source of equity funding can be the angel network. This term was adopted years ago to signify a large network of private investors who are willing to invest directly into early stage ventures.

In the past, entrepreneurs found angels through networking and word of mouth - a difficult and arduous process at best. Today entrepreneurs have the advantage of the Internet with over 1,780,000 angel sources. These are just four sites with which I am somewhat familiar: Midwest Investment Network (www.midwestinvestmentnetwork.com),

Go Big Network (www.gobignetwork.com/funding), Angelsoft (www.angelsoft.net), and Network of Business Angels and Investors (www.nbai.net).

Professional venture fund financing at the very beginning "seed level" will be elusive. One may find private investors who, because of personal or other connection, might consider helping at the seed level.

Here are some quick statistics to consider from, Angel Investing for Entrepreneurs: Early Stage Funding for Long-Term Success by Susan Preston (John Wiley & Sons, 2007):

· About 35 percent of private investing is done at the "startup level" (some sales developing) and only 18 percent at beginning seed level.

· Of the investment that does take place at this level, 55 percent is less than $100,000 and 21 percent is between $10,000 and $50,000.

· Most private investors expect to be able to cash in by the fifth or sixth year.

· The majority of private investors became involved after a referral from a friend. Most like to invest close to home (to provide oversight and save on travel costs).

It also is important to understand how any particular deal is structured. The first time viewing a term sheet from an investor may be somewhat stunning and shocking. In it will be clauses, terms and words never before seen. To understand the nomenclature, I would urge reading: Term Sheets & Valuations—A Line by Line Look at the Intricacies of Venture Capital Term Sheets and Valuations by Alex Wilmerding (Aspatore Books, 2006).

Good private investors and venture capitalists will execute due diligence. Asking for clarification (and a copy of the typical due diligence questionnaire) early in the investment negotiation process will help ensure a comfort level with the type of research a potential investor will perform on both entrepreneur and company. Make sure that this questionnaire is all the information required.

I have known venture capitalists who will use this initial due diligence piece as a starting point, then continue to add to it over an extended due diligence phase while allowing the entrepreneur to dangle - not knowing if the investment will be approved. This allows venture capitalists to "test" the entrepreneur and see how he/she handles the added pressure. This tactic also allows the venture capitalist to secure better terms than initially agreed upon, so beware.

The primary piece is the personal due diligence, which will most likely weigh heaviest in the final decision. That means checking out all the key players and evaluating the personal skills each brings to the table. Customers will be the first contacted - their acceptance and satisfaction with the product/service will be critical. Professional service providers (attorney and accountant) also will be interviewed as will company suppliers. Credibility will rank very high in an investor's final decision.

Debt Financing

A last source of capital is debt financing. Commercial banks today may be impossible to consider for an early stage company even if early cash flows can be proven. Person-to-person lending through websites is another option. (Some websites are listed below.) Each site will list requirements for qualification. Personally, I have no experience with these online companies and for that reason, urge caution.

Person-to-person lending sites:

· www.globefunder.com,

· www.lendingclub.com,

· www.prosper.com, and

· www.zopa.com

There also is a relatively new credit source for small business that bridges the gap between traditional business loans and higher priced alternatives.

On Deck Capital (www.ondeckcapital.com) is, itself, a startup, funded by large venture capitalists. With the current tight credit markets in the U. S., it is a timely resource. It is geared to the business slightly beyond startup with some proven revenue flows. Lending criteria is based largely on a cash flow analysis of the business. On Deck Capital lends up to $100,000 to businesses that have been operating at least a year and can demonstrate credit card sales of at least $3,000 per month. The application can be completed simply and online. This seems to be a worthwhile alternative for the business that has been up and running for the required amount of time.

What Investors Will Want to Know

Once two or three investment sources have been identified, a company and its entrepreneur must prepare and position before the first contact is made.

Consider for a moment that when seeking financing for an entrepreneurial opportunity, support is needed from those who do not share the entrepreneur's passion. Aristotle wrote that there are only three ways to persuade others - logos, pathos and ethos, or in plain English, logic, emotion and character. That said, there are four key areas to be addressed are: management, business concept and technology, market and sales.

The most important of the four is management. The best business idea in the world cannot be implemented without competent people. In some cases, even a bad idea can be salvaged when there are extremely talented and capable people driving it. Every professional investor is well aware of the importance of an organization's management team and spending time here will not be wasted.

Management should be viewed in the broadest sense possible. It is vitally important for the entrepreneur to put in place a competent and experienced team. A venture capitalist will look for people who have worked together before, shown that they are able to get along in stressful working conditions and, perhaps, even completed projects ahead of schedule.

The entrepreneur also should give thought to the startup's board of directors and/or advisors. This will speak volumes about how willing one is to subject his/her ideas to challenge and accept change, if necessary.

A board of directors does not have to be large; two or three highly experienced and competent industry people are likely enough. (This does not mean the company's attorney, accountant or any of the entrepreneur's cronies.) A competent board consists of people who push and challenge - hold the feet to the fire, so-to-speak.

A board should not be too large to start. Most venture capitalists will want a board seat in return for an investment. Venture capitalists also may know, through contacts, valuable potential board members for consideration.

Finally, the last piece of management that will give strong indication of the seriousness of the operation is the professional team selected. An accountant and attorney both need to have had experience working with startup companies, preferably in the same industry. The same is true of the company's banking relationship. This may mean leaving relationships that have been established over time.

The business concept and any supporting technology both need to be solid and work. The venture must exhibit an ability to add enough value to product/service to gain above average margins for like companies. It is critical that price isn't the only reason for existence; added value will bring competitive advantage that cannot be easily duplicated by others.

When analyzing the market for a venture, solid knowledge is a must. Factors to consider include: the total market size; exactly who the customer is; how many of these customers have actually been spoken to, feedback received; the means by which customers will be reached; and how this company will be able to aggressively pursue this market.

Sales are a final consideration that needs to be addressed. Very few venture capitalists will wish to invest in a company that can't show a proven concept with actual sales. Exhibited high demand here with order backlogs or committed orders will go a long way to garner investment interest.

It should go without saying that all of this "compelling story" should be told in a succinctly well-written business plan.

Why Planning Matters

On August 22, 2008 Sramana Mitra wrote an article titled: Carts Ahead of Horses, which appeared on Forbes.com. This article retells the story of serial entrepreneur, Murli Thirumale, now working on his second technology startup. This second venture is faring far better than his first.

The first startup failed to verify the market for customizing computer content for mobile devices. Although he had effective technology, the timing was off and he found few customers. Ocarina Networks, his second venture, is doing much better because he first identified the need in the marketplace before developing the product. He now has coined a phrase, "SDBS," which stands for sell, design, build, and sell.

He obtained financing for his first company; although with limited proof of the market he gave away significant equity in the process. With proof of concept and satisfied customers endorsing the vision, investors are now coming to him. Thirumale has been able to retain a significant equity portion while still raising enough to fund his company.

Scar Tissue Event Seven: Establishing Sales
What do You Mean, Will it Sell?

A critical rule of entrepreneurship that seems too easily forgotten is that nothing can happen without sales!

One of the first questions that I ask the beginning entrepreneur is this: "If I or someone else would be willing to write you a check today to fund your concept who will be the first customer you will call?"

It may be hard to believe, but the usual response is, "I am not sure." Even worse, I have heard, "I haven't sought out potential customers because I am afraid of early demand, and I do not wish to have early exposure until I am really ready."

Many have taken the mistaken path of assuming the market. It happens far too often to be funny. The naïve entrepreneur will take a look at the potential overall market, which will naturally encompass at least the U.S., and, in some cases, the world. This type of assessment always identifies a huge market, so much so that the fledging entrepreneur assumes that if he/she obtained an infinitesimal percentage, it would yield more than adequate sales.

A market this large will be easy to slip in to, win all the sales necessary, and no one will be the wiser, thinks the entrepreneur. I can attest that in real life it never works like this. Market research conducted this way will positively not fly with the investment community.

It is critically important to know precisely who that initial customer base will be and fully understand how to reach it. Additionally, there should be exhibited interest from this identified market segment - at a minimum, letters of testimony stating interest in purchasing the product/service or better yet, some actual real life exhibited sales.

This seems so rudimentary that it is ludicrous to me that anyone would have the audacity to ask for money without this proof. A total understanding of the market and the ability to show that it actually exists are absolutely essential.

Scar Tissue Event Eight: Over Promising and Under Delivering
"All We Need To Do Is Get It Delivered"

As sales begin to develop, ensuring that everyone who is selling knows absolutely everything about the product or service being offered is essential. Every customer question should be anticipated and answered acceptably.

In the beginning, products may need to be placed on consignment, or the company may need to give limited use trials or, in some cases, give key customers the product for free in exchange for a written endorsement if they are satisfied. The entrepreneur might look for means to gain an introduction to a potential customer from a mutual friend. Finally, ironclad guarantees and backing the product fully with impeccable service are necessary.

Everyone has experienced the frustration with today's mega-sized consumer product companies that promise fantastic customer service after the sale. When attempting to access this "wonderful service," the customer often experiences an email that goes indefinitely unanswered, or in the case of telephone service, is given, by computer, a laundry list of choices that seldom fit the problem. Those who do persist in an attempt to actually speak with a live person are put on hold for a minimum of 20 minutes (This is my limit and I will hang up after that so I am not sure how long it would be if I waited it out.) only to be confronted with language barriers that make the experience even more exasperating.

The company, which promises impeccable service (with live contact), had better live up to its claims. This goes for anything related to the customer interaction/experience. Never over promise and under deliver on a service or product - it would be better to not make any claims in the first place.

Quality customer service is equally important to before-sale service. Order processing should be easily understood and accessible to the customer. It is essential that the order fulfillment process is timely and effective. Being able to deliver on the sales side with over and above efficient and effective service will go a long way to establishing long-term success.

Scar Tissue Event Nine: Poorly Designed Pricing Strategy

"We covered our costs didn't we?"

Frequently, an entrepreneur will devise a pricing strategy through surveying the competitive market. Then, since his/her company is a startup with lower overhead, decides market share easily can be won by undercutting the competition on price.

This business philosophy fails to recognize that within a short time, the young company will begin to acquire that very same overhead to support the growing organization - thus requiring a price hike at a time that may not be advantageous.

Another, usually destined for failure, strategy in pricing is what I call "bottom-up pricing" or "cost plus." The engineer, who has designed the next best thing, will typically utilize this method. He/she carefully lays out the production and distribution costs and then places some additional margin above that to establish the ultimate customer price.

I prefer to see entrepreneurs develop a "top-down" pricing strategy. The entrepreneur should: Begin by looking at all the added value the product/service brings to the market; try to look at every way the product or service is currently delivered and the applications; utilize knowledge accumulated about the market to improve where others have fallen short and created dissatisfaction in the customer base; try making the product/service better in every way possible.

Once that analysis is completed, compute (in dollar terms) exactly what the added value of the product/service will save the customer. This is the entrepreneur's added value and should not be left on the table. Adding 100 percent of that to the price of the product is not likely, but recoup as much as is reasonably possible. A "cost plus" pricing strategy will not recognize added value. A value-added pricing strategy will help justify a price above industry averages yielding above average margins and creating a shorter time to profitability.

It is always difficult to raise prices later after discovering that a far better price could have been implemented from the start. This flaw is recoverable but it can take years to regain the margins that could have been realized all along.

A customer price that is too low can also exasperate a company's ability to grow - leaving it short of cash to fund its development. It is always better to look at ways to justify an above average price and margin than to look at ways to be cheaper than all competition. The market will always meet a new price competitor. It is generally one of the easier threats to meet. A competitor with many added value features along with a higher price will tend to be ignored. Competitors find meeting added value is more difficult and time consuming.

Price can be a valid strategy; it is just extremely difficult to execute well enough to be able to impact a market. Customers today are quite jaded by price claims. Conventional wisdom suggests that, in order to make an impact with price, one has to better the lowest market price by 30 percent or more. This is nearly impossible for a start-up. If attempted, it will likely leave the start-up with smaller margins and thus insufficient cash flow for sustainability or growth.

So what is necessary for the development of a good pricing strategy? Let me offer some suggestions to start the process:

Work Backward. Talk with the final customer and gain an understanding of what he/she will pay. Try to understand, if the service/product will be displacing another one, what the customer is currently paying. Look for features that customers value highly and also discover why they buy the competitive product.

Add Value Every Way Possible. Improve quality in every way. Add special features and provide customization. Provide follow-up support, speed of delivery and state-of-the-industry service.

Educate and Develop the Customer Base. Provide training in product use, promote the added value features, focus on repeat sales and get referrals. Keep customers updated on product improvements, listen to customer input and provide a ways and means for easy customer contact.

Identifying the Customer – One Story

When I worked in the venture capital industry, I came in contact with a group of extremely brilliant engineers who had, at one time, worked with Seymour Cray on the development of the first super computer. After the demise of the supporting company, they formed a consulting engineering group.

In between contractual work, the engineers began to assemble a database of current and historical weather information from the National Weather Service as well as through access to government weather satellites. In total, they built a database with 40 years of weather information. This database enabled the partners to develop computer models, which greatly enhanced meteorologists' weather forecasting. This new modeling system was far beyond anything that existed. Meteorologists said that it was better than anything they had ever seen. Everyone involved believed it would greatly enhance the weather forecasting industry.

While innovative, early contact with this group led me to the conclusion that the "product" was not clearly defined. They needed an experienced entrepreneur to help them put together a saleable product. Even so, the group still managed to secure investment from a variety of sources. An initial round of investment provided just enough to get the product to "saleable" form before money ran out.

I was contacted again and with the great product presentation, coupled with the increased credibility of the current investor group, we added to the investment. Our money was used for developing the marketing and sales effort.

Even so-called "sophisticated" investors can experience a scar tissue event when they should know better, as was the case here. The meteorologists who were contacted in the early development stage were not the modeling systems' actual customers. The actual customer was the broadcast weather industry, most of which had developed its own models for televised use and, therefore, had no interest in purchasing something from anyone else. After months of trying, the company was unable to garner one sale and was rapidly running out of cash for the third time.

We immediately ceased all development work and sales effort. Employees began to talk with anyone that might have a use for weather information.

In a completely fortuitous turn of events, the company's CEO happened upon a conference for the wind energy industry. A breakout session discussion revealed that despite rapidly increasing demand, quick deployment of wind energy was impeded by the time it took to find a site. The process, which measured wind velocity over time at various altitudes, could take up to 18 months and cost several million dollars. Our CEO knew that, in our database, we had wind information that could predict wind supply over time with little modification. The company would be able to provide predictable wind data for any altitude in any geographic area in the U.S. This data could be turned around in a matter of weeks - not years - and for a cost less than six figures!

Following this meeting, the interest in our product grew. The only issue we had was our pricing had followed the old "cost plus" model with little or no consideration given to added value. After all, we would potentially be saving a customer several million dollars on their wind farm development – surely we could capture some of that in our pricing. We knew this would have to take place gradually, over time, delaying profitability by several years.

Wind Logics was re-launched and through the hard work and dedication of everyone, from the CEO down, it became a real success story. The hard work helped develop a rapid sales ramp up and the company was later sold to Florida Power and Light with a comfortable return to investors. Without that fortuitous attendance at the wind energy conference, this company might not have made it.

Luck does play a role in success but it would not have been needed if we had spent the time up front speaking with actual customers to see if they would actually purchase and use the product as originally designed.

Scar Tissue Event Ten: Failure to Cover All Legal Issues

"Why do I need an attorney?"

In closing this chapter on financing the entrepreneurial venture, it is important to remember that competent legal counsel can play an important role. Recall my earlier story about Cliff, who had a failed partnership relationship and the difficult time he had negotiating a settlement. If he had spent the time upfront drawing up both a partnership agreement and a buy/sell agreement between the two of them, things would have gone more smoothly. This is just one example of a situation where the entrepreneur can become entangled in legal matters that can, at worst, sink the venture and, at best, consume huge amounts of time and resources when neither can be afforded. It is always wise to find excellent legal counsel early on in the development of a venture. It is time and money well spent. When selecting an attorney, be cognizant of these issues:

Initial Business Structure

How will this startup be taxed and governed? Understand the differences and compare the consequences of a C-corporation, an S-corporation, a partnership or a limited liability company.

Relationships within the Business

The company will need agreements with all equity partners, non-compete agreements with key associates, employment agreements and buy/sell agreements.

Third Party Relationships

Personal guarantees, loan and investment covenants and, perhaps, landlord leases and supplier agreements must be taken into consideration. It is especially critical to fully understand and get legal advice on all financial agreements and their related covenants. These especially can come back to bite later on.

Fully Know All Related Regulation

The entrepreneur must be in compliance and fully understand the ramifications of all laws and regulations that apply to the industry.

Understanding the Fine Print. There is an old saying that "the devil is in the details." If there are "landmines" in any legal document, they will be contained in the fine print. The entrepreneur must make sure he/she reads everything and asks an attorney to explain anything that isn't understood... before signing!

Many entrepreneurs assume everyone is as honest as they are. Unfortunately, this is not always the case. Full and complete discussions on every aspect of the venture should take place. Everything should be spelled out in writing. If there is no meeting of the minds, there can be no enforceable contract.

Never allow an attorney to negotiate a deal; instead have them draft the pertinent documents afterward. Pay attention to verbal and written communications so they do not create binding obligations. And, consider the future as well as the present in all legal dealings. Always try for the win/win in any negotiation; in short "do the right thing."

It is always wise to be very certain that all legal matters are handled upfront in a competent matter. It will save untold heartache in the future.

Section Three:
Survival and
Growth

"Life is a great big canvas:
Throw all the paint on it you can!"
Danny Kay

Chapter Four

"I Can't Believe It, We Got The Money!"
"Are we having fun yet?"

Scar Tissue Event Number Eleven: Losing Perspective

"After All this I deserve new digs and a car!"

For many people the pursuit of a dream business is more or less all-consuming and, at times, never ending.

Along this journey there will be self-doubt. After multiple meetings and presentations, when the folks on the other side of the table who have the money all nod in agreement, it can come as a shock.

Suddenly, the entrepreneur must shift from seeking financial support to an implementation of everything promised in the business plan. It can be intimidating and humbling.

I have seen the issues surrounding this shift multiple times, having gone through it personally, as well as teaching about it and then spending time in the venture capital world. The transition is not always successful.

The entrepreneur has funding and now needs to prove to those who have invested that he/she can perform by implementing this wonderful business plan. If the business plan was done correctly (and self-written), the entrepreneur should be able to execute it in his/her sleep. Still, getting started is always a little scary.

There is a responsibility that comes with taking other people's money (O.P.M.). Now is not the time to go out and find new office space or buy a new Escalade. The occasional entrepreneur who acts as if he/she has just won the lottery always shocks me. Since this is normally an equity investment, which carries no interest, dividends or fixed repayment date, the money seems almost free. (I must warn, however, that in many cases today the outside investors may require a convertible preferred stock that will carry an interest rate and, thereby, obligating interest payments.) Nonetheless, there are countless stories of entrepreneurs who have literally squandered away early money on frivolous things.

My advice: Bury the ego early.

I have personally seen young startups rent space in high rent districts, buy new office furnishings, and/or reward themselves for the time spent raising money with a new car. These, or other lifestyle changes, are absolutely the wrong signals to send to investors. The more frugal one can be, the better. Unless there are customers who need to come to the office or business (like a retail store concept) an address is meaningless.

Squandering early money also can result in running out of capital too early in the game. The end consequence may be wasting precious time seeking more money, which can mean giving up more equity at a reduced valuation, especially if the concept remains unproven.

Time to cash flow is always critical. The shorter the timeline to cash flow, the better. Cash flow is synonymous with sales. That means that all the first money needs to be focused on getting sales - as soon as possible. I would make it a rule to evaluate each expenditure with a simple question, "Will this help gain more sales or achieve sales more quickly?" If the answer is no, then don't do it. Garnering sales as quickly as possible will help build both credibility and sustainability for a new business.

While working as a venture capitalist, I was contacted about an investment opportunity in home furnace technology. Research had been funded by, what was at the time, the Gas Research Institute - an industry funded research and think tank for discovering new technology in the natural gas industry. GRI had invested over $3 million.

At the time our venture firm looked at this opportunity there were no sales (red flag No. 1) and the CEO was Denver-based and working approximately three days every other week in Minneapolis, where the company was located (red flag No. 2). Since the company had been rather liberally funded from the GRI, there was no effort to conserve funds (red flag No. 3). The CEO had elaborate offices in Denver with a staff of two people and flew to Minneapolis first class (red flag No. 4). No effort had been made to define a precise application (defined as a product) for the technology (red flag No. 5).

Prior to the investment, we insisted on a new "qualified CEO" (someone with industry knowledge, experience and contacts) and also more accountability for how the money was spent.

An extremely qualified and competent new management team enabled the company to finally move ahead and develop a product that was adopted by an industry manufacturing leader. Because GRI owned the majority of the stock in the beginning they lost a major equity chunk with our investment, but the company survived and has done well.

Scar Tissue Event Number Twelve: Failure to Track Cash

"What do You Mean We can't Meet Payroll?"

As a company expands and grows sales, it is critical to carefully monitor cash flow. As stated above, the initial thrust is to get cash flow started. Once that occurs, it becomes essential to grow into positive cash flow. This means a lack of profitability in an accounting sense, but cash expenses are being paid.

The shorter the time to positive cash flow, the better. At the risk of redundancy, that means all the first money needs to be focused on attaining sales as quickly as possible. This is a difficult lesson to learn - so many feel that everything needs to be "perfect" before meeting the customer. Perfection is always something for which to strive, but for the entrepreneur, it may come further down the priority list.

Think about Microsoft. Has this company ever released a "perfect" piece of software right out of the box? The software always works and is functional but it also has bugs. Bugs can be so commonplace that one might wonder why they didn't spend more time working them out.

Long ago Microsoft recognized that in the competitive marketplace they operate speed to delivery is critical. For this company, it is better to come back with good support and fix later. A company should not commence initial sales with shoddy products or poor service. However, an entrepreneur should not become fixated on everything being perfect; perfection should be the aim yet at the same time one must realize it may never be attained.

Once again, careful cash management IS ABSOLUTELY CRITICAL! The entrepreneur and the company's credibility will be established, in part, through responsible management of investment money.

Three financial statements are needed. A P&L (profit and loss) is important to show sales and profitability and is needed for accountant monitoring of the tax situation. A balance sheet will be required by most banks to measure assets and liabilities as well as assessing net worth. The most critical statement and the one the entrepreneur should be most concerned with is the cash flow statement.

In the early days of the family grocery store business, my grandfather always had a "cash drawer," which he monitored on a daily basis. If the amount inside the drawer was growing he knew everything was okay. However, if it was not, he knew immediately that corrective steps were needed.

A more sophisticated approach is the use of a cash flow statement. At the start, I would suggest a cash flow statement be developed and updated weekly. As the company becomes more stable, updates can move to once each month. A cash flow statement should outline rolling projected cash needs for at least one year out. Each month, numbers should be adjusted to the actual and the forecast readjusted as necessary.

Use of a cash flow statement will help predict cash needs in advance. If money must be borrowed, negotiations can begin early, before the entrepreneur and the company are time-pressed. In addition, long-term use of a cash flow statement leads to better advance projections over time. The whole objective is to never ever run out of cash!

Cash Flow Conservation Tactics

In addition to monitoring cash flow carefully, every tactic must be employed to conserve it. I previously discussed some cash flow conservation tactics in the section on funding alternatives, but it may be useful to review again here.

Negotiating extended credit terms from suppliers, obtaining advance down payments from customers and bartering products or services for outside services/products are a few examples of ways to conserve on cash. In addition, it is imperative to stay on top of accounts receivable. Borrowing or renting equipment that is only needed a short time and outsourcing non-critical functions help avoid building fixed internal overhead. College interns or moonlighting professionals can be utilized for special projects.

Bringing the customer to the company can minimize travel expenses. A strategic alliance with a complimentary product can leverage distribution or create cross-promotional opportunities. Employees' relatives often are willing to moonlight, making calls to prospective distribution companies or organizations. The entrepreneur should explore every possible opportunity to avoid spending cash.

Always remember that from the minute one accepts "O.P.M." there are two masters to be served – investors and customers. A third will come later, as employees are added. This realization may come as a shock to those who thought entrepreneurship was a clear avenue to total independence with no one to answer to but oneself.

Building Skills, Building Credibility

The University of Chicago Business School recently completed a study, "Which CEO Characteristics and Abilities Matter?" by S. Kaplan, M. Klebanov and M. Sorenson, that showed that the most successful business CEOs were persistent, attentive to detail, had good analytical skills, set high standards and were efficient. Many who are entrepreneurial would probably not fit these standards.

Most entrepreneurs excel at oral communication, flexibility, enthusiasm, and general people skills - often known as "soft skills." To be able to add value and build a company, the entrepreneur will need to train and transition to competency in the so-called "hard skills." This is not an easy leap. But, those who do not make the transition may find themselves forced out of their own company. Those who are unable to build hard skills may want to consider bringing in a great C.O.O.

Why Smart Executives Fail and What You Can Learn From Their Mistakes, (Portfolio Publishers, 2003) by Sydney Finkelstein, a management professor from Dartmouth's Tuck School of Business, offers further insight on the pitfalls facing the entrepreneur. This work illustrates the importance of learning from failure rather than success and I highly recommend it.

Building on personal credibility in the early days is a must. Early credentials such as work experience, education, and the propensity to work hard can be added to work completed on the business plan and the persistence exhibited in pursuing this opportunity. Commitment has been shown by the entrepreneur's willingness to work long hours and sacrifice wages. Still, none of this is enough to ensure success.

Now, it is imperative to begin to develop the credibility of the opportunity, itself, and ultimately the organization. The beginning of organizational credibility is a comfortable ramping up of sales along with the expansion of the customer base. This demonstrates proven market acceptability, which, of course, is vital. At the same time, successfully broadening the channels of distribution and fine-tuning operational systems will go a long way toward establishing organizational credibility.

Distinctive competencies are vital in establishing long-term growth and stability. These are activities, skills or capacities that a business is uniquely good at in comparison to competitors. If honed and carefully developed, these grow into competitive advantages. A competitive advantage, then, is a distinctive competency that a customer will highly value and will use as a buying criterion.

A competitive advantage becomes a sustainable competitive advantage when a competitor cannot easily duplicate it. Sustainable competitive advantages are added value, which ensure sustainable, above average margins and profitability and, thus, long term stability.

Sustainable Competitive Advantage – Two Examples

A good example of sustainable competitive advantage can be found in Netflix, the online video rental company. Netflix has sophisticated software in place, which tracks rentals and then makes future rental suggestions based on past consumption. The company has multiple distribution outlets strategically located throughout the U.S. Viewed selections are turned around sooner than would seem possible (in some cases two days). A problem disc can be replaced through an online request – no questions asked. The mighty Wal-Mart attempted to compete and ended up leaving the market.

On a smaller scale, my friend, whom I introduced earlier, Nikki Robbins, with Peace of Mind Daycare, has established her own set of competitive advantages. She has a barber come once each week to give haircuts, arranges for laundry and dry cleaning services for parents and hosts a once a month parent potluck to discuss school events, issues and parent concerns. She has a pizza night along with games and once each month on a Friday evening, she sets up her activity room with roll-away beds, makes popcorn, and shows children's movies so parents can go out on a date. These are just a few of the added value/competitive advantages she offers to distinguish herself from others. Is it any wonder she has 300 children and very satisfied parents?

Growth and Adding Value

Growth is an issue with which many company owners struggle. Growth for the sake of growth doesn't accomplish much but most would acknowledge that no growth is, in most cases, not the wisest philosophy. So, how much growth is right? Then, how is that "right" growth best achieved?

Personal goals will help determine how much growth is desirable, although a modicum of growth should be achieved just to stay even. I also will assume that one of the reasons an entrepreneur starts a business is to create and accrue value that may be harvested at some point. This latter point, one of accruing value, is something I would like to further discuss, for growth can never be achieved without adding value. Therefore, it seems natural to start with the value creation process.

In the book The Value Growers, consultants McGrath, Kroeger, Traem, and Rockenhaeuser (McGraw-Hill, 2001) talk about the importance of having dual focus on both the top and bottom lines. Both are needed for value-added growth, they say. Too much focus on the top line will generally sacrifice the bottom line, reducing critical cash flow, making the critical reinvestment support necessary for growth hard to come by. Conversely, maximizing the bottom line generally will result in lost sales and momentum due to decreased competitiveness. Therefore, the two must be in balance.

This may be all well and good but it still does not clearly define value generation. What is it that creates value for any particular situation? Certainly new ideas for marketing, new products, improved quality, new and/or different market niches, cost controls, greater internal efficiencies, new product applications and uses, etc. All of these can add value to a company and build growth. In addition, however, the customer transaction, itself, is also of key importance.

Earlier, I talked about the importance of elements that comprise building a loyal customer base by providing good customer service. Good management at the transactional level is a critical part of this service. One needs to analyze everything that comprises this service.

In The Myth of Excellence, by Fred Crawford and Ryan Mathews (Cap Gemini Ernst & Young U.S. LLC, 2001), the authors isolate five elements of every business transaction - price, service, access, product and experience. Even great companies do not try to achieve excellence within each element. It is better, say the authors, to focus on being dominant in one element, better than the average in a second, and as good as everyone else on the remaining three.

Here are better definitions and greater perspective of each element taken from the authors' interviews with more than 5,000 consumers.

Price

Believe it or not, low price was the lowest priority for the customer. Many people have become jaded by low price claims that turn out not to be true. Consumers want a fair and honest price consistently delivered. Customer research has shown that, today, those who lead with price need to be 30 percent lower than the competition in order to make an impact. That is difficult, if not impossible, to do consistently.

Service

Unexpected value-added services are an effective means to building customer loyalty, which result in business value growth. However, caution is advised here. This focus requires above average service at every step in the transaction.

Access

Today, access is less about location and more about convenience. Parking, being able to locate the product desired once there, and probably, most importantly, easily shopped space. It also means: Cleanliness in all customer-accessed areas, especially restrooms; neat and orderly spaces; hours designed to fit the customer's lifestyle and, finally, it means that the final purchase is handled quickly and efficiently. (Could these consumer desires explain why the Internet is becoming so popular?) Long checkout lines are not desirable. Finally, the business must be open at the customer's convenience, not the owner's convenience.

Product

Customers equate product with consistency more than anything else. Again, exorbitant claims over time have resulted in a cynical consumer. If this element of the transaction is chosen as a focal point, the company must provide solid products that work and are easily available at all times - no out-of-stocks. It's as simple as that.

Experience

People desire common courtesy. They wish to be treated fairly, honestly, respectfully and feel that their business is appreciated. The authors stress the importance of establishing a sense of intimacy and trust. Customers do not want to be "tricked" into buying something more than they really want. They also want to deal with product-knowledgeable people.

One focal point in this work stands out; customers are tired of the old means of selling. They do not have the patience or time to endure a long transaction process. The business that makes them feel that they are appreciated, values their time, and offers consistently good products/service will go a long way to building a loyal customer base. With that comes growth and added value for a company. As simple as it all sounds, I have found few entrepreneurs who have learned to provide good customer service well.

Scar Tissue Event Number Thirteen: Failure to Develop Systems and Controls

"What do you mean we're disorganized?"

Achieving financing and establishing a growing sales curve are by no means the end to establishing sustainable long-term growth. Sales growth, itself, can lead to failure in the company not organized to handle it. Every company or business needs to become "professionalized," implementing more formal systems, procedures and controls.

Professionalism can be partially defined by the following:

Knowing the Numbers

This means constant cash flow analysis, planning and forecasting for capital needs. Good cash controls and regular financial reports with comparative analysis are musts.

Know Asset Needs

Stay efficient with the proper application of current technology, good inventory controls (growth and turnover) and knowing when to lease versus buy.

Know the Customer

Who are they, what do they value about service and/or product, what are their needs, what additional things should be done to keep their business? A business cannot exist without customers. An entrepreneur must have a passion for finding customers, keeping them and ensuring they are serviced in a timely and consistent manner.

Know Competitors

Visit them, study them and shop them. Stay on top of the worldwide industry. Follow what is new and copy what works. Know industry/competitor strengths and weaknesses.

Know the Market

Survey customers regularly, develop customer feedback systems, be responsive and find and explore niches. Constantly try different distribution tactics. Play with different channels, pricing strategies, different packaging techniques, and different advertising methodologies. Track everything and keep a database of results. Check out Microsoft's MapPoint, which can assist here.

Know and Follow a Plan

Be sure to have broad participation in the development of the plan and then follow it, changing it only when conditions warrant. Update it annually.

Know and Constantly Improve Quality

Low price is not always the right way to access a market. Price without quality will not garner repeat customers. Look for added value that the customer appreciates to bring them back. Make sure to deliver workable products or above average services every time.

Develop Effective Management Systems

Monitor key metrics, develop a sustainable culture, develop incentives, delegate workload equitably, and share authority.

Of course this all sounds magnanimous and simple, but this potential scar tissue experience is one that occurs all too often. Without professionalized systems, an organization or business cannot grow beyond the limits of the entrepreneur's personal control.

Measure Key Metrics, Avert Disaster

Knowing numbers can assist greatly when monitoring various aspects of any company. In today's fast-paced economy, having ways and means to track various aspects of the business allow the entrepreneur to recognize changes that may have negative impact down the road. Metrics should be easily accessible, quickly recovered, and nicely quantifiable. They also should be relatively simple and limited to no more than five critical variables. Measurements, when intelligently applied, will not only save time and money but may have the potential to save a business.

I once met a businesswoman who could recognize potential pitfalls with a phone call. She owned a very successful manufacturing company, which at that time was generating annual revenues of $250 million. At breakfast one morning, I watched her excuse herself to call the office for a morning report. With this simple call, she knew the number of sales calls the day before with the amount of sales closed, the amount manufactured (including rejects) and the number of orders fulfilled and shipped. This data, although not very financial in nature, was all she needed to spot developing problems.

However, analysis may need to be more sophisticated.

There are software packages that assist with drilling down the business database for information critical in decision-making. Business intelligence (BI) software is designed with many applications in mind. BI software can run upwards of $50,000 installed and can generate more reports and data than one could ever find the time to read. Much thought is required to get the right selective, analytical data from a company's database. Here, there is a risk of simply overwhelming everyone with meaningless paper. The old "garbage in garbage out" rule still applies.

There is a market in the small to medium-sized business for good measurement information and there are some reasonably good and economically priced packages available. Since BI is such a broad area, measurement and report parameters must be set. Here are some considerations:

Product Analysis

Develop reports of individual product sales/profitability, the customer profile, where the product is purchased, number of returns, etc.

Cost Analysis

Determine the cost of building each product, or the cost of distribution of individual products. A service business could compare the varying cost of delivering a particular service across different customer groups. What is the optimum customer support level to generate the most profitability? Monitor gross margin across product groups.

Customer Analysis

Develop an exact demographic profile of the customer base. Identify the most profitable customers and find out what turnover might be. Are there purchase differentials between existing and new customers? Look at how varying advertising might affect product sales distribution and what factors might influence more profitable purchases. The average sale per customer, number of repeat customers and age of receivables also are factors not to be ignored.

Sales Analysis

How does the weather affect sales? Are there regional differences in how a product/service is purchased? Look at how varying competitive conditions affect sales. Monitor inventory turns, on-time deliveries, market share changes, new customer growth, reorders, etc. Sales mix changes over months or seasons or product lines, etc. also should be evaluated.

Internal Analysis

Of course, monitor cash - particularly differences between projected and actual cash flow. Look at employee turnover to industry norms and monitor any budget to actual discrepancies.

Metrics should be limited to between five and 10 - measured on a weekly basis. Metrics selected should be easily recoverable and serve as early warning signals when things go wrong. Metrics are only good if they are used, hence there is a need to keep them simple, selective and precise. All previously mentioned indicators are important to watch but not all need to be monitored as closely as the key ones. It also may be good to develop additional metrics, which are only reported on a quarterly basis.

I have a few final thoughts on metric worth noting.

Companies such as SAP (www.sap.com) and SAS (www.sas.com) are both looking at serving smaller clientele. SAS particularly is good with companies that need heavy-duty statistical analysis. These small business products are worth evaluating.

Specifically designed small to medium size business BI solutions were reviewed in PC Magazine several years ago. Four different companies' BI software was evaluated: Micro Strategy 7i (www. microstrategy.com), Brio.Enterprise 6.2.2 (www. brio.com), Cognos Power Play (www.cognos.com) and Crystal Enterprise 8.0 (www.crystaldecisions. com).

PC Magazine determined that MicroStrategy's 7i was the most easily deployed of the four tested and was named editor's choice. Brio's product required a new language to be able to take full advantage of the program. The Cognos product was the closest to "plug and play" and was more modular by design than the others, said PC Magazine evaluators. Finally, Crystal had the most extensive package but the reports generated were harder to understand and not as easily generated.

Such evaluations are useful, but before considering any of these more sophisticated business intelligence packages, careful consideration must be given to needs and in-house ability to continue to support the software to keep the data updated and relevant. These are much more sophisticated information tools than the average smaller business would probably ever need, but might merit consideration for the fast-growing business before things spin out of control.

"There can be no happiness if the things we believe in are different from the things we do."

- Freya Madeline Stark

Chapter Five

"Why Is It That I Have To Do Everything,
Can't Anyone Think For Themselves?"

What is a management culture?

Scar Tissue Event Fourteen: Failure to Develop Long-Term Management Practices

"If it is to be done right, I will need to do it!"

Once the product/service is proven acceptable to the marketplace and some sales and sales growth are achieved, the entrepreneur is immediately faced with more work and decisions than can be comfortably handled. At times, the demands are overwhelming. This is a critical juncture, particularly if the organization is to be built beyond the limits of personal control.

Matthew Bender & Co., an international business consulting firm, suggests taking stock before hitting the panic button. Questionnaire feedback from associates can offer insight on perceptions of one's management style. The suggested questions to ask are below:

Are my instructions clear, or must you spend time trying to figure out what I want you to do?

· Do I change my mind often and ask you to alter your assignments after you've already started working?

· Do I often edit or make changes in your work without really improving it?

· Am I open to new ideas?

· Do I often seem disappointed in your work?

· Is my criticism usually constructive?

· Do you feel you can trust me?

· Do I help you develop your skills?

· Am I usually available when you need help?

· Do I operate in a crisis mode too often?

These 10 simple questions can usually quickly assess the root of the problem. I realize it is not comforting to gain honest appraisal from associates. However, continuing in the same operating mode may soon result in acquiring the scar tissue event mentioned at the start of this chapter. Driving away talented people with vital skills to the venture also is a significant risk. Should that happen, this scar tissue event moves into the fatal flaw category.

Growing the Organization, Growing a Management Style

The skills employed when starting a business or organization are much different than those needed to successfully grow it. The entrepreneur is the one who set down the venture's core values. Hopefully, there are others in the organization that share in those values. The entrepreneur who has surrounded him/herself with those with like-minded values is at least part way home.

A directive style may have been necessary to get the organization to this point, but now the time has come to think about how to succeed and grow long-term. The ultimate objective is a level four firm: the organization has a fully developed product/service, many satisfied users and a fully developed market. It also will have a fully staffed, experienced management team that works well together.

To build an organization that seems to the outside world to operate efficiently and harmoniously is no easy task. The key, to start with, at least, is to survive (or avoid) this scar tissue event, which is usually brought on by an inability to delegate.

A manager who ran one of my operating units had this problem. It ended up costing him his career and moved him from a recoverable scar tissue event to a fatal flaw. When I finally stepped in this individual shared with me that:

· He could do it better himself

· He did not have the time to spend teaching others

· He did not trust or have confidence in his people

· He was afraid of losing control (and power)

· Basically did not know what he could delegate. In interviews with his people, I found out that they all had a nickname for their manager. They called him "Little Jesus."

This situation can be easily avoided. Stressing trust in employees is imperative. Trust is one of the most powerful motivational tools that can be employed and is absolutely required to build a sustaining organization. Begin by:

· Stressing results, not details

· Don't be sucked in to the trap of providing solutions to associate's problems - simply turn their questions around

· Establish measurable and concrete objectives

·Develop and establish reporting systems, dead-lines, parameters, and realistic deadlines.

· Grant the necessary authority and flexibility that will allow them to do their job

· Do not baby-sit but allow them to do the job their way.

This last point is the most difficult. It is very easy to over-correct to make sure things are done "your way." But, remember that delegating relieves some of the responsibility and failure to do so serves as a great disincentive for employees. I can almost guarantee that if associates are allowed freedom, the job will almost always get done – and, perhaps, done even better.

Those who find developing advanced management skills overwhelming may want to consider putting a professional board in place. A solid and experienced board can help guide and offer advice in critical decision-making. Such a board also can demonstrate additional credibility to the outside world. However, there are matters to consider when developing a board.

Consideration must be given to the type of skills a board member would need. I would suggest avoiding current professional advisors (attorney and accountant) – the organization already has (and is paying for) their advice. An initial board should be small in size, somewhere around five people is sufficient. Experienced people with the requisite business expertise and people who can offer objective independent advice are preferable. A board prospectus that lists desired qualities and capabilities should be developed. The purpose, goals and expectations for the board should be laid out as well as the structure, function, compensation, term limits and time demands. A separate overview of the company's current status along with the business plan summary and vision for the future also are important.

A board should have gender, age, cultural diversity and areas of expertise balance. Candidates can be found from interviewing the company's accountant, attorney, suppliers, bankers, as well as the entrepreneur's current mentors. The entrepreneur, then key team members should interview each potential board member personally.

ScarTissueEventNumberFifteen: Misapplication of Style and Roles

"We were having morale problems, but now we are constantly missing our budget; What do you mean we need a management system?"

I have always disliked the term "professional management" as it brings to mind hierarchy with its commensurate top-down control. I prefer to use the term "entrepreneurial leadership" to distinguish my preferred style from the previous one. After all, wouldn't most of us prefer being "led" to being "managed?"

Now with that being said, I do need to add a caveat - the "leadership and management paradox." Not many organizations can survive a "pure" application of either style.

Traditional management principles describe the role of manager as one of execution, operations, planning, budgeting, controlling and problem solving. These are all very necessary for organizational success. In contrast, the leadership role tends to be one of setting goals, identifying mission, and in general, energizing, empowering and enthusing people.

Both skill sets have a place and too much use of one may come at the expense of the other. Here, balance is key. An organization with a strong leader who has little or no management skills will risk failure due to inefficiencies, waste, inability to meet budgets and deadlines, etc. The organization with strong management and no leadership will be faced with a rudderless organization - one with morale problems, no unifying, motivating goals and one likely to miss opportunities for growth.

A close friend of mine believed in rigid top down management control. No one was allowed to make a decision without first consulting him. Still, employees were severely reprimanded if things went wrong - he would blame them for poor execution. After years of this management style, he drove away those people who were competent and was left with very few skilled workers. This business managed to survive multiple generations yet it ultimately and tragically failed as a result of poor management.

I have learned through my 40-year career journey that in today's times OLD STYLE HIERARCHICAL COMMAND WILL NO LONGER WORK! (I highly recommend this be written down in indelible ink some place as a reminder.)

The nature of work has changed. In the early days of our economy, large parts of the job market were filled with unskilled work, repetitive tasks, single-skilled jobs, functional-based work, etc. Today's jobs are much more focused on multi-skilled tasks, knowledge of work, teamwork, project-based activity, customer power, coordination among peers, etc.

The new work contract demands that people be treated differently. People often work because they want to, not because they have to. Technology has forced much of this change and will continue to impact how organizations are structured and led. People are rapidly becoming the only truly sustainable, competitive advantage because technology is constantly eroding most others.

Today there are three key macro tasks essential to developing an organization's entrepreneurial leadership. These are: 1) strategic vision, 2) organizational development and 3) managing the corporate culture.

Kate Ludeman in her book, The Work Ethic (Dutton Publishing, 1989), writes the following: "Home is where the heart is. And the heart must come to work, if we are to meet the expectations of the new work force. More than ever before, people expect to find their worth affirmed at work. Twenty years ago, not even 5 percent of our population expected to develop their potential and find satisfaction through work. Today, 40 percent of employees believe they have a fundamental right to self-fulfillment, to develop and use their intellectual and creative abilities to the fullest. They believe that they are worth as much to the company as their managers. They want to perform meaningful work that brings value to the world, and they have the latent power to insist on being treated as worthy."

This quote has a tremendous amount to say to those companies/organizations interested in successful growth and, I suppose, it also has a message for those who fail to listen. While we watch many of our major institutions fail across the country today it helps us to begin to understand, at least partially, why this may have occurred.

Many years ago, I had an opportunity to read a book by Robert Greenleaf titled Servant Leadership (Paulist Press, 1977) that really helped me rethink the way I dealt with people who worked with me. I recognized that my style needed to change if I wished to be effective, not just efficient. The article forced me to rethink how I looked at my position and encouraged me to look differently at hierarchy in associated organizations.

Proponents of servant leadership advocate turning hierarchy upside down. The term "subordinate" can be demeaning. The role of an organization's leader/manager is one of support, not the other way around. A leader needs to ensure the organization has competent people who share in its value system. People should receive the training, tools and other resources to be efficient and effective in their roles. The leader/manager can accomplish this by openly sharing information, being approachable, honest, open-minded and a good listener.

Management always should look for ways to remove obstacles, or "de-motivators," that prevent people from doing a good job. People respond more productively to that than any incentive one could dream up. Good leaders/managers: Ask people what they need to be more effective and efficient, supply those things and then stay out of their way and let people do their job the way they know best.

Entrepreneurial Leadership – One Example

Entrepreneurial leadership is exemplified in the work of Murray Harpole, a friend whom I met while teaching at the University of St. Thomas. Harpole documented his story about the founding of Pentair, Inc., which today is a $3.5 billion diversified manufacturer of water treatment equipment and protective products for electronics and electrical equipment.

Pentair has over 16,000 employees worldwide. It is truly an entrepreneurial success story. But in 1966, when it was formed, it consisted of five engineers and pooled resources of $26,000. The goal was to build a company that would design and build balloons and inflatable systems. Soon the money began to dwindle and so Harpole knew they needed to raise more through a stock offering. Through much trial and error, they were finally able to raise $18,500 but it cost the company dearly. At the end of the offering, the founders were left with 17.6 percent of the company.

The sales side of the business did not come together as planned, but Harpole was able to put together a deal to acquire American Thermo-Vac, a company that formed large plastic parts for things like canoes, shipping containers and golf carts. It was a difficult transaction and since American Thermo-Vac was in almost as desperate a financial condition as Pentair, it took some creative work to get the deal consummated for $50,000 with half down.

Due to haste, the deal lacked normal due diligence. Harpole soon found out that the majority of assets acquired had creditor liens against them. At one point, creditors had the sheriff seal the door of the factory and attach all of the assets. Still, somehow they were able to close out the first year of business with sales of $30,000 and a loss of $100,000.

In the second year, the newly merged company was able to use the thermo technology to develop a line of canoes and began to see some real sales growth. However, the canoe business was proving to be an industry in which it was difficult to make a profit. Harpole's board pushed him to close it down while his bankers were suggesting he liquidate the company and close it completely.

In the nick of time, Harpole heard of a paper mill owned by Peavey that was for sale in Ladysmith, Wisconsin. The company manufactured single-ply toilet tissue. The plant was in disrepair and the company's reputation had been damaged by a series of labor problems. The mill was close to bankruptcy but, nonetheless, produced 50 tons of paper and sales of $3.5 million a year. A purchase was negotiated to pay $10,000 down with another $20,000 to be paid at the end of one year and 20 percent of after-tax profits for five years. The new owners assumed all liabilities. Again, little or no due diligence was done and Harpole compounded his earlier scar tissue by later finding out that the company had debt of about $1.4 million. Harpole saw to it that three key people got stock in the new entity following the acquisition.

Because of his personal lack of knowledge about paper manufacturing, Harpole soon realized how dependent he was on each and every worker. He made it a point to meet with all, admit his lack of knowledge and explain just how close the business was to bankruptcy. He asked workers to use their expertise to turn the business around and told them to only come to him when they needed something that would help them do their jobs better. The company was making a profit by the end of the first year.

This was the beginning of a management philosophy that put Harpole in good stead throughout the balance of his career. Pentair went on to become a holding company comprised of several paper mills when the board recognized that it might be good to diversify. Over several years, the mills were sold off and other companies were acquired as Pentair grew into the diversified manufacturer that it is today.

Pentair's management still follows those early principles established by Harpole. Company headquarters houses fewer than 100 workers, which is surprisingly small for a company of its size. Each company manager of the portfolio of companies that it owns is given wide discretion and authority to run his/her own business. Headquarters is there to provide support and guidance when asked. Very few diversified companies like Pentair would consider the role of top management to be one of support instead of command, but that philosophy aided in building a multi-billion dollar company from such humble beginnings. Further details of the Pentair story can be found in Harpole's book, Living the American Dream (St. Thomas Technology Press, 1992).

Making the Case for Better Management Practices:

The book, ...And Dignity For All (Unlocking Greatness with Values-Based Leadership) by James

Despain and Jane Bodman Converse (Financial Times Prentice Hall, 2003), describes how Despain, a vice president of North American plants for Caterpillar, came to an epiphany in his career and improved his management style for the better.

Despain had been the typical hard-nosed boss who believed whole-heartedly in command/control leadership. This helped him become a feared boss but one who "got the job done" his way - period! He rapidly climbed the corporate ladder and landed an assignment in Japan. While in Japan he began to compare his leadership style to that which he saw exhibited there and developed an appreciation for the development of a culture of performance and respect. He began to see how his style would, at times, create divisions and huge rifts between people. The end result of division was a negative impact to productivity.

Upon returning to Caterpillar U.S.A., Despain decided to transform himself. He developed a set of nine openly communicated core values. These were: trust, mutual respect, teamwork, empowerment, risk taking, a sense of urgency, continuous improvement, commitment, and customer satisfaction. He asserts that these values were the blue print for setting boundaries for employee ideas, giving workers the freedom to make decisions, and the ability to make a difference.

On June 28, 2009, the Society of Human
Resource Management reported the results of its
annual employee satisfaction survey. This multi-
faceted report can be found at: www.shrm.org/
surveyfindings. The study found that only 51 percent
of employees were satisfied with their company's
communication, 50 percent were satisfied with the
work itself and 45 percent were satisfied with their
company's culture.

Practicing Good Management Skills

Jeffrey Pfeffer, a professor of organizational
behavior at Stanford University, has written more
than a dozen books about the impact that people
can have when used as a strategic advantage. When
teaching entrepreneurship at the University of St.
Thomas, I brought Pfeffer in to speak to students
and also the outside entrepreneurial community on
this topic.

At St. Thomas, we used his book, Competitive
Advantage Through People, (Harvard Business
School Press, 1995) in one of our courses. In it, he
documented companies, like Southwest Airlines,
Plenum Publishing and Tyson Foods, which through
intelligent management helped to develop their
people into a key strategic advantage. His latest
book, What Were They Thinking, (Harvard Business

School Publishing, 2007) deals with the scar tissue that happens when people are considered expendable. In this latest work, he assesses what happens when wages, staff and benefits are arbitrarily cut in order to meet ever-increasing profit targets. The resulting loss of talent, reductions in service and innovation end up exasperating the situation and result in further sales reductions.

So what does this all look like summed up? I believe that a good entrepreneurial leader today would practice the following:

Complete Open Book Management

This means sharing all key information, data and knowledge to help people understand the company/ organization and how they contribute to its overall success. (This is one of the most difficult concepts for entrepreneurs to grasp.) All I can say is that those who try it will never go back. No secrets! This will demonstrate trust in the organization's team, empowers employees and promotes loyalty.

Offer Challenging Work

People today enjoy change and challenge. In order to successfully grow, people must feel that they are a part of an organization. The effective leader will allow choice and participation in decisions about change and new opportunity.

Offer Individual Growth Opportunities

Everyone likes to learn new jobs and see future opportunity. Cross-training and expanded educational opportunity should be a part of every company. Reimbursed educational costs also should be a policy. Be sure to exhibit continued respect for the individual.

Offer Gain Sharing

In any company/organization, everyone - if they are doing their job - helps that company grow and add value and should have a right to share in that additional created value in some way or fashion. This can be achieved through phantom stock or actual equity participation. As far as I am concerned there is no more powerful motivator than equity. Cares and responsibilities also become easier when shared with multiple owners.

Inspire through a Clearly Articulated Vision, Clear Values and Trust

Besides writing these down, a company and its leaders must exhibit them by modeling in every day activities. Allowing people to have authority to act independently in accomplishing their job will build trust within the organization.

Fun

This may seem to be a strange practice for any company/organization today struggling just to survive. Yet time and again, examples abound of extremely productive companies/organizations that are able to still enjoy work and even have fun. Celebrating successes, be it individuals or corporately, help people feel appreciated.

Recognition and Pay

Recognition is one of the simplest ways to gain a loyal group of associates and a simple "thank you" costs nothing. There are other ways in which employees can and should be recognized - flowers and cards are in order for special family events and as are rewards for long-time service. Pay disparity should be avoided at all cost. It will be noted if an owner takes a salary many multiples over and above what anyone else makes - no matter how "secret" one might think it to be. The business owner who uses his/her company as a personal checkbook will leave others feeling cheated and shortchanged. Compensation must be open and equitable. For owners, a return on personal investment in the business beyond salary can be easily explained and understood.

There are other works on this topic that I highly recommend. Jack Stack, CEO of Springfield Remanufacturing Corporation in Springfield, Missouri wrote two works The Great Game of Business (Doubleday Publishing, 1994) and A Stake in the Outcome: Building a Culture of Ownership for the Long-Term Success of Your Business (Bantam Books, 2003) His first work details how open-book management turned his business around. His second work explores creating a culture of ownership and how he accomplished this in Springfield.

One last work worth reviewing is Open-Book Management: The Coming Business Revolution, by John Case (HarperCollins Publishers, 1995). This book looks at the application in even broader detail and shows a greater range of companies that have applied it successfully.

I will close on the topic of open-book management with this final bit of food for thought. A five-year study by two Harvard professors, James Heskett and John Kotter, compared the performance of companies with open, participative cultures against those that did not have such a culture. Interesting statistics were revealed in their book, Corporate Culture and Performance, (The Free Press, 1992). In terms of sales growth, openly managed companies out-performed the others by a factor of more than four times total revenue growth. The openly managed company's employment growth exceeded the others by almost eight times and net income was more than 700 times greater over this five-year period! (Quite impressive.)

It can be a hard thing to do, but trust me...it works.

Scar Tissue Event Sixteen: Failure to Build a Sustainable Culture

"Now what is a culture?"

Throughout this book I have hoped to show techniques that will allow an entrepreneur to construct a business/organization that will be sustainable long after he/she has left.

The job of creating sustainability is never ending and creating organizational culture is one aid in the quest for longevity.

Webster's New World Dictionary defines a culture as, "the ideas, customs, skills, arts, etc. of a people or group, that are transferred, communicated, or passed along, as in or to succeeding generations." It is important to develop, hone and carefully craft this culture. Failure to do so will result in a less purposeful culture developing on its own.

Building morale and work quality is a part

of establishing and managing a culture. With an acknowledgement of redundancy, I would suggest the following could help with that task:

- Setting standards of personal integrity.
- Giving people opportunity to do what they enjoy by building on their strengths.
- Challenging people by giving them assignments that stimulate personal and professional growth.
- Giving people space to take initiative, volunteer new ideas and attempt new things.
- Having tolerance for mistakes. The first mistake is always a learning experience.
- Recognizing ability and promoting accordingly.
- Telling the truth—compulsively, immediately and repeatedly.
- Setting goals around measurable outcomes.
- Never criticize—only validate.
- Watching what is said—being explicit.
- Establishing agreements—don't rely on expectations.
- Not attempting to manage what can't be measured.
- Taking written notes and confirming to others in writing.
- Trust...but verify.

Conflict can be managed effectively through:

· Tolerating mistakes and allowing people the right to "not know."

· Respecting differences of opinion and allowing people to disagree with management.

· Always explaining reasons for decisions and policies.

· Always listening attentively.

·Never permitting conflicts of personalities— keep encounters about work task-centered, and personalities out of the discussion.

In addition, the manager/leader must address feedback:

·Providing clear and precise performance standards.

·Praising in public and correcting in private (an old one but still true).

·Looking for solutions rather than assigning blame.

· Developing a culture of self-esteem.

· Avoid over-directing, over-observing and over-reporting.

An organization's culture should address rewards systems by recognizing people often and simply.

Such an organization allows people to have fun and encourages them to learn and grow.

Those who follow the guidelines listed will go a long way to building that sustainable culture that will last long after the entrepreneur has left the building.

Scar Tissue Event Seventeen: Sloppy Hiring Practices
"We need help NOW, find me a warm body!"

It is impossible to build a quality team if the modus operandi in hiring is to "just find someone to do the job." Two critical things follow from careless hiring practices. First, is that many incompetent people can end up on the payroll, thereby, increasing the pressure to oversee these associates and; secondly, the organization runs the risk of providing less than efficient service and top quality.

A recent book, Who, by Geoff Smart and Randy Street (Ballantine, 2008), addresses how to assess and hire the right people.

"Hiring the resume" can be a mistake, assert Smart and Street. The entrepreneur may find out later that the individual does not live up to what's written on paper. The authors stress implementing rigor in the hiring process through multiple interviews over several days and at different times of the day and with different people involved. Trusting a "gut reaction" should be avoided when hiring. A quote from Wilma Askinas says it best: "Never mistake personality for character."

The authors contend that close to 50 percent of business success is the result of finding the talent that fits the situation. A trial period, with no commitment for either party, can work well in situations where there may be doubt.

Unfortunately, many spend more time reading the daily paper than on hiring a new employee. Yet customers will judge daily a company based on their interface with its employees.

Spending time on the front end of a hiring decision is much easier than trying to rectify a bad hiring decision after-the-fact. I have met few managers who are quick to recognize bad hiring decisions and when they do it takes some time to correct the situation. In the meantime, good customers can be lost. Most good managers do not enjoy firing someone they hired because they are admitting they made a mistake and because it is not a pleasant task.

I have an example from my own personal experience that underscores the importance of good hiring practices. Recently, I had the privilege of interacting with the switchboard person at a company that I deal with on a fairly regular basis. (Enough so that I would hope I would be considered a good customer.) When I called, I asked for a particular department and this person very graciously put me through to that telephone. I was then put on hold for 10 minutes. I hung up and called back a second time and asked the receptionist if there was anybody in that department. The response was: "How should I know? I only answer the phone." I was put through again for another 15-minute wait. On my third call back, I complained that no one was answering that phone. I was told: "What do you expect me to do? Go back there and see if anyone is around? I imagine that they are busy with customers!" My call was again forwarded for a last five-minute wait before I was able to explain that I was a customer.

How does an organization avoid this situation? Often, when I think of a successful company, the first attribute that comes to mind is the organization's "great people." Those "great people" did not get there through lucky happenstance. Good employee teams are carefully cultivated and developed through a conscious effort.

Good hiring decisions and practices are an essential part of leading and managing...in fact in many ways these are essential components of competent leadership. Treating people ethically and fairly, along with the critical importance of training and developing teams are all elements of evolving a great company culture to which people enjoy giving a part of their life.

To develop great people, one must start with good people. Is it easier said than done? A few suggestions might help with the recruitment and selection of the kind of people who will make any entrepreneur proud of his/her company.

Believe it or not, I suggest considering nepotism. Chances are that an excellent employee may have close relatives who share the same qualities. If qualified people are hard to find, offering retraining programs also is worth consideration. A local vo-tech college can assist in developing programs that train people with needed skills. Recruit early - perhaps as early as high school - to begin building interest in the jobs the company offers. Offering college internships can provide an opportunity to try out qualified people.

Selection is even more critical than recruitment. It is an area where many fail under pressure to fill positions. In spite of time pressures, an organization and its leaders must be very selective, conducting multiple interviews, checking references closely and utilizing trial initiation periods. As stated earlier, people with shared values make great teams. It is vital to take time to determine if a candidate is a good fit.

I have had many entrepreneurs tell me that this is impossible. People are too good at hiding their values, they say. I do not agree. Those who are selective and follow careful procedure in the interview process will minimize hiring mistakes. A book by Lou Adler titled, Hire with Your Head (Wiley & Sons, 1998) can offer further guidance.

The Hiring Process – A Few Guidelines

First and foremost, I urge caution in using the quick first impression as a means to a hiring decision. Time must be spent with an individual to determine how he/she might fit any given organization.

Many experts suggest beginning with a short telephone interview to qualify the person for the job. This prevents making a quick decision based on physical appearance alone. As much as I hate to do this, it is best to use a written list of questions to avoid missing key points. Written questions are recommended for both the phone conversation and the face-to-face interview.

After the successful completion of the qualifying phone interview, a face-to-face interview should be scheduled. The entrepreneur must remind him/herself that this selection is hopefully a long-term employment relationship. The "right" employee will be someone who will relate well to others on the team and someone who will be a great representative of the company. Devoting the necessary time will result in a happier decision for both employer and employee.

The personal interview will be far more effective with questions that require thoughtful answers - not just a "yes" or "no" response. Don't ask, "Did you enjoy your last job?" But rather, "Can you give me an idea about what you do in your present position and can you describe for me how you have made an impact?" The interviewer should focus on the present job and ask the candidate to discuss how they would handle the responsibilities and what they view as the most important measurements of success. An assessment by the candidate on past job performance, based on recognition for job performance, is also useful. Interview questions always should recognize the specific needs of the organization.

Values, as I said, are difficult but not impossible to determine. Here are a few questions, which are also value indicators: What are their hobbies? How do they spend leisure time? How do they like to be evaluated? What are key performance measurements that would indicate success to them? What do they think makes for a great place to work? How might co-workers describe working with them? Have they ever been reprimanded in a job unfairly and how did they react? How do they describe their personality and are there traits here that might help or hurt on the job?

Finally, I will offer a few interview technique tips. The interviewer must be sure to listen. Allowing for some uncomfortable pauses, and not feeling responsible for filling all available airtime, will force the individual to respond to questions. Adequate time, at least two hours, should be allotted to avoid rushing. Performing reference checks ahead of the interview will likely generate further questions. (Reference checks are essential and be sure to use more than the list provided by the candidate. I will ask someone on the list if they know of anyone else that I should talk to about the individual.) And, as mentioned previously, multiple interviews with various team members are essential to ensuring a good, long-term fit.

Scar Tissue Event Eighteen: Failure to Develop a Work Team With High Morale and High Performance

"Why can't we keep people?"

When one thinks of extremely skilled leaders/managers, I believe one word that comes to mind is trustworthy. Nothing will destroy effective operational leadership (or lead to greater employee dissatisfaction) more than a lack of trust. Very simply, trust is key to making implementation of a strategic plan possible.

Trust inspires confidence, without which, suspicion reigns. Today's business headlines on executive salaries illustrate this point. It is not always the dollar amount that makes executive compensation packages so obscene, but the spread between the average person's wage in the organization and that of the high-salaried executive. It is hard to imagine that anyone can actually believe that the single reason for an organization's growth and added value is its top executive.

When viewed in the context of servant leadership, one can see that such outlandish compensation is the antithesis. It will foster distrust in the organization. An organization epitomized by trust will be more efficient and cost effective. Productivity goes up and costs go down in an organization where people trust.

I recently reviewed a book that spurred me to address this topic again. The book, The Speed of Trust (Simon & Schuster, 2006) authored by Stephen Covey addresses organizational trust and how it impacts the ability to execute. He writes that the traditional formula of: strategy x execution = results should be written: (strategy x execution) x trust = results.

This book is essential reading for anyone interested in having an effective organization that develops real long-term value for its stakeholders.

Covey asks readers to first ask themselves who they trust and why. Then, secondly, he poses a more provocative question, "Who trusts you?" Character and competence play a critical role in trustworthy people.

Covey discusses five fundamental waves in developing trust:

- Self trust
- Relationship trust
- Organizational trust
- Market trust
- Societal trust

The defining principle in the first one is credibility, established through development of four key things:

- **Integrity**- Built by keeping commitments, standing for something and being open with others.

· **Intent** -Very simply, this involves three things: a motive that shows concern for all constituents, an agenda that seeks mutual benefit (a win/win) and behavior that always acts in the best interest of others.

· **Capabilities** - Knowing oneself well enough to be able to run with strengths, stay relevant and envision a clear course for the future.

· **Results** - Take responsibility for results, portray an expectation of success and always finish strongly.

The second "wave" is totally about behavior. Covey advocates a "trust account" into which one must place an equal amount in 13 categories to come across as a trustworthy person. The categories are:

· Talk straight - share intent, be honest with all and do not manipulate

· Demonstrate respect - through fairness, kindness and civility

· Create transparency - tell the truth and do not obscure

· Right wrongs - go beyond an apology by making restitution

· Show loyalty - give broad credit to others and do not speak about people behind their back

· Deliver results - develop a track record of accomplishment

· Get better - through continuous self-improvement

· Confront reality - do not duck hard issues but take them head-on

· Clarify expectations - through a shared vision and upfront buy-in

· Practice accountability - holding all involved (including oneself) accountable

· Listen first - take time to listen to other people first before giving advice

· Keep commitments - keeping all commitments should be a symbol of honor

· Extend trust - to all in the workplace

Covey defines the third wave as Organizational Trust. Nearly everyone has been involved in an organization with low trust. No one trusts anyone, so information is withheld, new ideas are not shared, people lie and cover up facts. This climate is totally debilitating to an organization and it eventually freezes into inaction. Systems and policies that are extensive and burdensome will foster this sense of distrust.

The fourth wave of trust is Market Trust, or the

broader community's views about the company's products/services and overall reputation. Finally, the last wave is called Societal Trust. It is closely aligned with the fourth and is grown and developed over time through exhibiting intent not just to take, but to give back to the community and society.

On a larger scale, one can see how all these waves of trust play out when looking at the current scene of corporate greed. There are not only excessive pay packages but also investment bankers and equity funds that buy companies, not to add value to the people of the organization or to society as a whole but, rather, to manipulate through financial structuring to maximize their own financial return. These types of practices have left some very good companies burdened with debt and top notch people without jobs or retirement benefits. It is easy for those of us that run smaller, private companies to cluck our tongues at such egregious behavior while in small ways practicing it ourselves. The entrepreneur must do everything possible to develop an organization around trust. In the end, it will be much easier to manage and the reward will be added long-term value.

A camper and large motor homes dealer who I knew very well was fortunate enough to start his company about the time that the first "boomers" were retiring.

Sales were great and he was able to attract some excellent sales talent. One of the dealer's associates had even been named the No. 1 salesman of a particular brand of motor home in the U.S. The salesman was very proud of his accomplishment but his employer never mentioned it or acknowledged it in any way.

Not long after receiving the award, this sales associate's father had a sudden heart attack, became critically ill and required major surgery. The salesman took some time off to be with his father. Upon returning to work, no one asked him about his father. Not long after, he discovered that his paycheck was short $100 per week. This took place after a record year.

After inquiry, the salesman was told by the owner that he determined the need to make more profit, so he arbitrarily cut wages to achieve it. Needless to say, within a year, the majority of the better people had left this dealership to work elsewhere. The dealership's sales fell precipitously and it is struggling to stay in business.

Good people are the greatest asset a company can have. To not recognize this on a continuing basis is the best way I know of to ensure failure, at worst, or a major scar tissue lesson, at least.

Section Four: From Sustainability to Immortality

"*Try not to become a man of success
but rather a man of value.*"
Albert Einstein

Chapter Six

"Finally We are Profitable, Now What?"

("When do I get a vacation?")

This is the place where, after all the struggles, the organization seems to have turned a corner. Things are certainly easier after the company is consistently profitable but the demands on the entrepreneur may seem to be never ending.

This is a critical juncture in the development of this wonderful opportunity. This is the place where the venture can hit a wall and never progress beyond it or the entrepreneur may choose not to continue and simply sell the creation and walk away.

The point has come where the entrepreneur must decide if he/she will undergo one more managerial transition. From this point, the entrepreneur must become less hands-on and more of a "keeper of the culture and overseer."

There are countless entrepreneurs who enjoy the chaos and ambiguity of the earlier stage business and recognize that their skills are not necessarily applicable in the later stages of growth. A perfect example of this phenomenon is contained in this passage from an October 6, 2008 Wall Street Journal article: "The departure last week of a Facebook, Inc. co-founder highlights a cultural shift that the Internet company faces as it tries to navigate the path from scrappy startup to big business."

In the last chapter we dealt with issues surrounding early success and the development of the organization beyond that of the one person led event. Shortly after that little bump in the road to sustainability, one will arrive at a juncture where consistent profit will lead to less concern with survival but greater concern about what happens if and when the entrepreneur leaves.

Perhaps, by now, the entrepreneur has wisely come to the realization that he/she is not infallible, omnipotent or immortal. So then, what are the next steps to potentially achieving immortality for the company?

Assuming the entrepreneur is not stepping aside, further development of the people in the organization is warranted. Those who followed the suggestions in the past chapters will have already assembled a competent team. Care and feeding of this wonderful asset will then need to become an even greater focus.

After a successful run to date, the entrepreneur will realize there are people in the organization that he/she does not know. Business matters are no longer resolved over a cup of coffee. In order to maintain the "old culture" there are things that need to be inculcated into the company to assure that the organization can continue to grow, evolve and succeed in the long term.

Let's look at the things the entrepreneur will be facing if he/she chooses to move ahead. These changes are not earth shattering change, but subtle efforts that can help the organization achieve a life of its own.

Communication

This is at the heart of any business success. Complete open and honest communication is critical with anyone involved in and with the business. This means that there are no secrets. Period. Amen! It is critically important. I also will discuss this as a scar tissue event later.

Responsibility

The entrepreneur alone takes responsibility for critical issues and problems that arise. There can be no blaming others, finding excuses or trying to cover up.

Give Credit

Although responsibility is assumed for the "tough" stuff, the entrepreneur shares liberally with those involved when the good things happen.

Focus

The entrepreneur cannot be distracted by anything! Things like new and different opportunities - unless they specifically add value to the product or service - have no business taking up time prior to achieving goals.

Customers

No business can exist without customers. This should not have to be mentioned except it is unfortunately forgotten time and again. The entrepreneur must have a passion for finding and keeping customers!

Add Value

Look for ways to continuously add value to the product or service. Trying to do something new at least once each year offers "surprise" to the customer base. Customer communication can offer insight on which added values really are desired.

Constantly Hone Sustainable Competitive Advantage

The entrepreneur must improve and constantly develop competitive advantages and be flexible, changing them when they no longer work.

Value People

It goes without saying that business owners, in most cases, are dependent on people they work with to deliver the proper service and/or products to the customer. The "Golden Rule" applies to associates. They should be treated as carefully as customers.

Foster and Develop Trust

This was discussed in the last chapter, but needs emphasis. A major ingredient missing in many companies is the trust factor. I speak with many business owners who feel that it is difficult, if not impossible, to trust the people with whom they work. Trust is something that, of course, has to be earned but, in many cases, even when people have earned it, they still are not trusted. There is a dividing line between the owner/manager and the other team members. Too often, the working environment becomes one of "us vs. them." True success will never be attained if that attitude prevails. When people are trusted they work doubly hard to maintain that trust. When someone is told that they are "trusted," it serves not only as a tremendous motivator but also as a way to empower people to take initiative. When that happens, great things can occur.

This last point deserves further comment as I can envision a question in the minds of readers already. "How do you ever begin to develop that kind of trust in today's rough and tumble world where loyalty seems to be a word that is never spoken?"

If one spends any time listening (really listening) to the other members of the organization, I believe it will become apparent that distrust is a result of either a lack of information or, worse yet, misinformation.

Trust has to start first and foremost with the entrepreneur and that means being totally open and honest about every piece of critical information that is used to run the organization. Yes, I am back to "preaching" about the importance of "open-book management" and being forthcoming with answers to questions that associates may have.

In the book, The Five Dysfunctions of a Team (Jossey-Bass, 2002) the author, Patrick Lencioni, claims that every time there is a problem in an organization it can be traced to communications issues. An honest, inward look at one's own organization may reveal the truth of this assertion. Another work with further insight is Practice What You Preach by David Maister (The Free Press, 2002). Maister focuses on the importance of empowerment and commitment to employee satisfaction in building a profitable and successful organization.

Trust in any organization can be further enhanced through employing the concept of servant leadership, which was discussed earlier. This concept was shown to work in an interesting experiment on the television news program 20/20 with John Stossel.

When it comes to managing companies, servant leadership is a concept most company owners find difficult to accept. Yet, there is proof that it works. Interestingly, the television show 20/20 with John Stossel aired an episode on October 17, 2008 during which he discussed some of the concepts of self-directed groups of people. Stossel interviewed economist Russ Roberts, professor of Economics at George Mason University. His latest book, The Price of Everything: A Parable of Possibility and Prosperity (Princeton University Press, 2008) describes how prosperity is created and sustained, and the unseen order and harmony that shape our daily lives.

The program's theme demonstrated that, oftentimes, government policies and regulation do nothing to promote greater efficiency and productivity. In fact, quite often and without controls, people seem to muddle through.

Stossel went to a public ice skating rink to illustrate. The host noted all age groups and skill levels were present on that rink yet all were managing, in their own way, to skate around the rink without outside direction.

Stossel then injected himself into the scene. With a public address system, he attempted to direct the skaters to skate more efficiently and in better order around the rink. The result was utter chaos. He then hypothesized it would be better if they used a skating "expert" to do the directing. He asked professional figure skater, Brian Boitano, to attempt to better organize skaters. The same confusion and chaos occurred.

This is much like the flight of a group of birds, which fly in perfect harmony without a "leader" telling them when to turn or how high to fly. The same concept is exhibited in schools of fish, in ant colonies and in other places in nature. This concept is known as spontaneous order or self-direction.

> Management that over-controls and over-directs is not efficient management. Intelligent people can do as well or better if left to their own devices. I know from my own experience that less directive management and more supportive management works better. Good people want to succeed. Excessive rules and policies take away all initiative, incentive and fun from the job. (Now, if we could convince government of this, wouldn't we all be better off?)

Empowering Employees, Building Trust – My Own Experience

Recently, I had the opportunity to work with two entirely different companies with which I have been personally involved for some time. These two companies are in two different industries and distinctly different stages of development. Yet, lately, both have struggled with a slow down in sales growth.

A common first reaction (at least it used to be mine) when times are tough is to look at every way there may be to slash expenses. The reaction from associates is likely the same I received. A "here we go again" attitude is coupled with a lack of cooperation. There likely is no extended effort on anyone's part to pitch in and help. In short, there is a lack of buy-in, stemming from a lack of trust.

In one of the two companies, the sales struggle stemmed from new and intense competition. The management team was tired and frustrated. Meanwhile, through all of this, every key person had been kept fully informed of the status of the company with every kind of information available, including complete financial statements. Many would believe that by doing this key people would "jump ship" before it was too late. Not one did!

Associates were concerned and wanted to work together to solve the issues. In private, and then group meetings, top management assured each and every employee that the solution would not be top down. A pool of money was set up to make physical changes in equipment or any place else where additional resources might enhance sales or productivity. Each person was asked to think of ideas and submit them, recognizing that the pool of money was limited.

During group meetings all ideas were discussed and consensus was reached on the use of funds. Due to the limited pool of money, no one was able to get everything he/she desired. But, everyone got something. Associates left those meetings with a sense of empowerment, support and a sense that we are in this together and we will solve it together.

Since this was one of my own companies, I can relay that results have been positive. Within a year this company was back on track with positive sales, a record year of profitability and not one job lost. People are excited to be a part of the solution. The spirit of cooperation and sense of teamwork has never been better...even though times are still tough in a competitive sense.

There is empirical data to back this personal experience. Bob Nelson, the author of an extremely popular book titled, 1001 Ways to Reward Employees, (Workman Publishing Company, 2005), conducted a survey of 2,400 employees in 34 companies and found that most employees crave communication, involvement and autonomy.

Managing does not have to be onerous and lonely - not when a team with a sense of shared responsibility has been developed. A team works with, not for, the entrepreneur.

This does not excuse the entrepreneur from providing a competitive pay scale. But committing to these other non-tangible benefits effectively and passionately will temper the need for excessively high pay scales to attract the best and brightest. (That said, it is always beneficial to monitor the pay and benefits of competitors to stay on the leading edge in any industry. "Core benefits," i.e. health insurance, sick leave, vacation, etc. must at least match the competition. Then, look beyond at the softer benefits available in the marketplace. This can be accomplished through Internet searches on competitor's websites, interviewing former employees and viewing job postings.)

Employee Education and Training – A Means to Employee Satisfaction

A discussion about the cultivation of a high performing workplace and retaining a quality workforce would not be complete without mentioning education and training.

The average career person today will experience six to eight (depending on the news source) career changes in a lifetime. I am in my third major career life change. Along with those major changes, I have experienced about three or four minor ones. Some of these changes, including the current one, have required that I learn new skills. This means re-education, which becomes more difficult as one moves through life.

I also have had the opportunity to work with the development of hundreds of people. I have always preferred to develop people from within as opposed to trying to go outside to find new people to fill new positions. Over the years, I have found this to be to be highly valued and appreciated by the people with whom I work. It's been a great morale booster.

In addition to a normal desire of most people to learn and grow, there is workplace impact caused by the rapidity of change brought about by technology and telecommunications. With today's tight labor market, it is imperative to do everything possible to train internally, keep employees up to speed and keep key people challenged and happy. Personal development can be a critical factor in any benefit program and can go a long way to promoting long-term employee retention.

In rural areas, education and personal development are always more difficult. Access to education can be difficult at best. In the past, many entrepreneurs would either grab educational "snippets" through weekend seminars, which, in many cases, would require expensive travel, or would send away for written material and attempt self-teaching. I remember attempting to save money by getting training for myself, then coming back to my business and personally training fellow team members. Again, this proved to be costly and time consuming.

Today, many of those limiting factors can be eliminated with online learning opportunities. A recent Merrill Lynch study claims that in 1990 it cost $300 for an average hour of traditional business classroom training, but by 2005, this cost was reduced to $0.03 through electronic learning. There are no longer geographical restrictions. In addition, some studies have shown that people taught online have the advantage of working at their own pace leading to higher retention.

Sounds like the ultimate solution to workplace continuing education and skill development doesn't it? Unfortunately, the industry is still in its infancy. Not everything will be found on the Web or in convenient CD ROM format. With some effort, I have discovered that there are numerous institutions that provide a variety of higher education opportunities online. These vary from a few courses to full-degree university programs. Since we do not have room to list all of these, I will just mention a few as a starting point. These are randomly selected and no effort was made to evaluate their content or their ability to deliver.

Capella University (capellaeducation.com) - Offers a portfolio of non-degree courses.

Takeaclass (takeaclass.com) - Offers continuing education, professional development and life-long learning courses.

TrainingNet (trainingnet.com) - Develops an online marketplace for individuals and businesses to find, evaluate, and buy training and education.

University Access (universityaccess.com) - Provides online education through partnerships with several postsecondary institutions.

Wyncom (wyncom.com) - Offers lessons in leadership and provides communication and leadership skills from authors and speakers.

Many of these companies are private and relatively small but their products are new, innovative and refreshingly different.

In addition, there are the online corporate training programs that tend to focus more specifically on training and skill development. This is a more diverse group and a cross section is listed.

Click2Learn (click2learn.com) - Innovative learning for IT and business professionals.

DEPC (depc.com) - Developer of custom information systems training software with an extensive library of ready-to-use computer-based training and self-study products.

Headlight (headlight.com) - Develops simple, quick access to hundreds of online courses. Subjects include team building and business communication.

Pensare (pensare.com) - Helps organizations innovate best practices, gain access to business expertise, and improve strategic performance through the power of intranets and desktop application software.

Adayana (adayana.com)....Provides custom Web-based training applications and enterprise consulting for online learning.

I would suggest that industry peers, trade associations, and suppliers can point to other education and training opportunities. I also would spend some time learning about the content each has to offer to ensure a good fit.

Scar Tissue Event Nineteen: Lack of Honest and Forthright Communication

"How Do All These Rumors Get Started?"

A recent visit to a friend's company included a tour and a chance for a nice dinner that evening with key members of the management team. During dinner, one of the vice presidents happened to mention that there were rumors running around the company that they were in financial difficulty and about to be sold.

The CEO was flabbergasted. The company had a fairly good previous year and was on track to do much better in the coming year. He was frustrated and quite visibly upset by this rumor. I was planning on staying over, so after dinner I asked the CEO if he would have breakfast with me the next morning. He agreed to meet.

I told my friend, who chaired the board, of my plans with the CEO. I felt he needed to get to the bottom of this matter. He started the company from scratch and was planning to someday sell it to his management team. He had no intention of selling it to any outsider.

The next morning at breakfast, I asked the CEO if they had a large issue with rumors in the company. He confirmed that rumors tended to run rampant. When I asked him why, he didn't seem to have a good answer. I questioned him further, inquiring if he was aware of how the sale rumor started. He replied it was likely conjecture that evolved because of the age of the owner, who had no heirs and was spending winter months in Florida. It didn't take much imagination, concluded the CEO, to surmise that he was on his way to retirement and since he had no heirs, he had to be selling the company.

I asked the CEO if he was aware of the owner's plan to sell to the management team. He responded that he was not. I asked him how he communicated to his management team and then, how they, in turn, communicated to the balance of associates. He said there was no formal communication system in place. The management team met as necessary and the CEO would just ask them to pass along whatever policy changes or major decisions were decided upon to those who needed to know.

This lack of a formal means of communication was, no doubt, the catalyst for the internal rumor mill.

I made a suggestion to him that had worked for me in the past: Develop an informal "board" comprised of selected management and non-management team members.

Membership on this proposed board should no more than 10. Memberships would rotate, with each holding terms from one to three years, so that all seats would not turn over at one time. This board would not hold any formal power, but would serve as a sounding board and make recommendations to upper management.

At the same time, upper management would give the board complete briefings and reports of all company matters, including financial statements. (Oh yes, this is part of the "open book management" system that I spoke of earlier.) Furthermore, upper management would promise not to make any critical decisions without first getting input from this board.

The CEO had doubts, but I had the privilege of

pre-selling the owner on the concept. The gravity of the rumor mill issues made some sort of change imperative.

One year after implementation, everyone involved was impressed with how well this new advisory board was working. There were doubts and suspicions on both sides initially and the process required much time to get everyone up-to-speed on understanding corporate issues, financial statements and establishing trust.

The transition of ownership to the key management team went off without a hitch three years later. A key to success was the commitment on the part of management to be totally honest and provide any and all information requested by the "board." Those who implement a similar system will need to learn to listen, question, and then act on board recommendations. If management cannot, reasons need to be explained in detail. When implemented, this system will break down the barriers between management and associates - guaranteed!

A recent book from Warren Bennis, Daniel Goleman and James O'Toole titled, Transparency: How Leaders Create a Culture of Candor (Jossey-Bass, 2008) delves into this subject in great detail. The authors suggest that with today's digital technology it is nearly impossible to keep secrets within organizations. Since "secrets" leak easily and rumors do so much damage, it is so much better to develop a culture of candor within any organization. Openness is paramount to being able to build significant added value to a new venture.

Employees as an Organization's Greatest Asset – One Example

I would guess that many readers, like myself, have read, heard or said the following: "People are our greatest asset!" I would hope that those who use this expression also believe in it. Most value creation comes from the coordinated effort of everyone in an organization, not just the owner/CEO.

Aaron Feuerstein of Malden Mills (inventor and manufacturer of Polar-Tec) in Lawrence, Massachusetts would agree. In December 1995, a fire destroyed his company. Shortly after the fire, Feuerstein met with his 3,000 employees and announced he would continue their salaries for 30 days while he decided what to do.

Thirty days became 90 as he arranged for temporary facilities. The total cost of supporting his people after the fire came to $25 million. Prior to the fire his plant output was 130,000 yards of material per week. In temporary facilities it rose to 230,000 yards!

People asked him why at age 69, he did not simply retire. He replied that he couldn't abandon the people and the town of Lawrence. He also said, "The fundamental difference is that I consider workers an asset, not an expense." This certainly was apparent with the phenomenal productivity improvement.

In November 2001, Malden Mills filed for Chapter 11 protection from creditors. Many issues forced the bankruptcy filing, not the least of which were the expenses associated with building a new plant and restarting after the fire. Once again Feuerstein, then 75, was asked if he was going to give up. He said "No, "and at the insistence of the court, added management help. On Aug. 6, 2002, Malden Mills announced it was emerging from bankruptcy.

Morley Sather interviewed Feuerstein on 60 Minutes, the CBS news magazine, and asked him why he did it. His response, "because it was the right thing to do," resonates with me. I'm not sure how this perspective would play with the financial wizards and top corporate managers on Wall Street, but I believe there's a lesson here about good management that seems to have been lost on the current generation of wealth grabbers.

Evaluating Intangible Assets

There's much discussion today about the value of

intangible assets (like people) on company balance sheets. Traditional accounting methods haven't done a good job of recording these assets. Meanwhile, all of us who have owned and managed a business know that without our fellow team members, not much value creation happens. As we spend time and money for training and development, we enhance the contributions of team members and this certainly adds to their ability to add value to our enterprise. How to measure such value on a financial statement, though, seems to continuously elude accountants.

Looking at the human side of the equation is just one aspect of intangible asset valuation. An Internet search will reveal about 50,000 entries devoted to the topic. There are issues such as licenses, patents, copyrights, and, of course, today's hot topic on the valuation of options, granted management. Most companies use a methodology called the Black-Scholes Option Pricing Model to value options. It's not the easiest tool to apply in the real world and many experts dispute its validity.

Satisfying the accounting and financial services world that the value assigned to intangible assets is accurate is a major problem for business owners. I suggest that if an owner/CEO believes the firm has value in its intangible assets, he/she explores ways to measure and account for it - if for no other purpose than to satisfy personal belief. Will the company's money sources accept that value? Probably not immediately, and it will mean the need for a separate balance sheet. But, the additional value claimed will serve as a reasonable argument in the next round of discussions with investors.

So where does one begin to assess value for the intangible? The infinite array of resources available on the Internet can be mind-boggling. Many Internet resources are consulting firms that may charge more than a small company can afford. I first urge reading the book, Valuation of Intellectual Property and Intangible Assets by Gordon Smith and Russell Pary (John Wiley & Sons, 3rd edition, 2002). Other resources can be found at: www.valuationresources. com/Publications/Intangible.htm

Most large accounting practices also have methodologies to help with valuation of intangible assets.

My sense is that this discussion will be ongoing and I can only guess where it will end up. But, those who believe there is value in the intangible assets of an operation, should start keeping that separate balance sheet and use it to extend the debate every time in every meeting with the financial community.

The development and growth of a firm's intangible

people assets are a huge responsibility and this should be an essential role of the entrepreneur in this stage of a firm's development. It can provide much fulfillment, satisfaction and certainly enhance the sustainability of the company that she/he founded.

Generation Y's Impact on Entrepreneurship

Today's upcoming generation (often referred to as Generation Y) is demanding an open and honest workplace more than any generation before. Since not much is accomplished without people, serious consideration must be given to an open and honest workplace in order to recruit and retain this workforce.

An Oct. 13, 2008 article by Shelly Banjo appearing in the online Wall Street Journal did an excellent job of describing Generation Y. The article estimates that Generation Y made up 25 percent of the workforce in 2007. Naturally those numbers will to continue to grow.

This generation often chooses a supportive work environment over salary. Unlike past generations, they are not as enamored by Fortune 500 names as they are by meaningful work assignments and responsibility. They demand better feedback on their work and desire a more personal touch from their employer. A young entrepreneurial company will have the advantage when it comes to providing these intangible benefits over the large, mature company.

In the third installment of the Intuit Future of Small Business Report (please see www.intuit.com/futureofsmallbusiness), there is an expansive discussion of a massive research study that was undertaken by the Institute for the Future. This is an attempt to "identify, analyze and forecast the significant trends and forces impacting small business over the next decade." The report discusses the impact that technology is having on economies worldwide.

Cheap and easily available technology, states the report, is fostering the re-emergence of an artisan society. Generation Y's familiarity with technology allows them to be involved either as entrepreneurs or as a part of early stage start-up companies. Their desire for independence and constant reinforcement coupled with tech-savvy skills makes this generation of workers excellent candidates for entrepreneurial ventures. They are great at multi-tasking, creativity and have a desire to be a part of new innovations. The Intuit report predicts that Generation Y will have its greatest impact in entrepreneurship. Any up and coming entrepreneur would be wise to read this report to begin to understand how this new generation can become a part of a new venture.

Scar Tissue Event Twenty: Improper Benefit Package

"Why doesn't anyone appreciate what I do for them"?

If Generation Y is the round peg in the traditional square cubicle, then it is likely safe to assume that the traditionally crafted benefit package alone will not be a fit for this emerging workforce.

The unique qualities of Gen Y should be carefully assessed in order to design a benefit package that not only keeps them on the payroll, but also challenged, excited and happy. Standard benefits are a starting point, but the small unique "extras" in the package can provide a workplace "cool" factor.

A great place to look for a benefits package model is Google, where many Gen Yers would love to work.

Google provides a stress "chamber," impermeable to light and sound, where employees can go in and lie down to reduce stress. The company also boasts a slide to allow employees to navigate between floors. The lunchroom is open all the time with choice of food and drink at no cost. Pool tables and video games are available in lounge areas. Private soundproof cubicles (they call them "cabins") allow employees to attend to personal affairs. There are white boards scattered about the hallways and office spaces where people can jot down ideas. Every employee has two large screen monitors in his/her office space. Computers are maintained/repaired in a separate tech support center and employees can have a snack while waiting. Professional masseurs/masseuses are available as are a large room with subdued lighting, a massive aquarium and massive massage chairs for relaxing. There is a large library for reading and/or studying. Google also offers free laundry machines, a child daycare center, dog-friendly offices and an on-site doctor. By the way, the people who work there helped design and decide on the amenities.

These are the type of extras that today's generation is coming to expect. Google may be a little over the top, but at the same time, many of these benefits are not expensive to offer. I know of other companies that offer amenities such as a "surprise" free makeover, a gift certificate for dinner out with a spouse or special friend and one firm even has a day at a go-kart track.

I used to have a monthly lunch with about six associates at a time. These were special events. Each person would get a personal invite from me and we would go out to a very nice restaurant. Discussions were open and free flowing and everyone knew they would be considered confidential.

Multiple small awards can be the answer to this generation's desire for lots of feedback. One company uses a point system where managers can award people points for jobs well done. Points can be accumulated then redeemed for small gifts like a gift card to an electronics store.

Gen Yers also like to have mentors assigned to help guide their career at the company. This can be easily implemented by assigning senior team members to take their "mentee" to lunch (on the company's expense) periodically to see how things are going. Flexible working hours are extremely important along with flexible time off to be able to attend to family matters. Remember, it is not about money necessarily, simple and frequent recognition with a simple "thank you" will do.

Turnover is costly, which is something we all know but somehow fail to fully grasp. Talent is critical to success and constant turnover will most certainly hamper growth and development. Turnover should be monitored and compared to industry norms - 50 percent or less of industry standard is desirable. Exit interviews can provide insight (and possible guidance on corrective measures) if turnover is on the rise.

Companies, which strive to be known as a great place to work, will never have trouble attracting the talent that is so critical to success.

"The key to a leader's impact is sincerity. Before he can inspire with emotion, he must be swayed by it. Before he can move their tears his own must flow. To convince them he must himself believe."

-Winston Churchill

Chapter Seven

"So Far so Good, What's Next?"

"Aren't we finished yet?"

At this point, the entrepreneur and organization have been able to cross that large chasm from uncertainty to success. Adaptability to change is still a prerequisite for continued success, however. This is the point where I recommend a book by Sydney Finkelstein titled, Why Smart Executives Fail (Portfolio, 2003). It is a book particularly suited for this stage of development. In it, the author has identified seven habits of spectacularly unsuccessful people - mistakes best to avoid. These seven are listed:

· Seeing oneself and one's company as dominating the environment and, hence, not worrying about   responding to environmental factors that could have an impact.

· Becoming so closely identified with the company and product that self-best interest and company-best interest become intertwined.

· Having all the answers and making speedy decisions without sufficient input - in essence, being a control "freak."

· Consequently, expecting everyone to be 100 percent on the "team" and eliminating anyone who isn't.

· The ego is tied up with the company image and, thus, the owner/CEO spends too much time as the spokesperson and/or being out front.

· Treating difficult obstacles as easily overcome when, in fact, they are not.

· Falling back on earlier strategies/tactics that worked in the past.

At this current stage of development the entrepreneur will have moved passed those issues of the early startup. Market acceptance has been won and a new set of issues is beginning to emerge. There is increasing pressure to further develop management talent in order to properly handle the needs of this rapidly growing organization. Execution must continue to improve to gain market share. The importance of timely order fulfillment, superb service, efficient operations and top quality control is evident. Everything dreamed about is beginning to happen yet there is still self-doubt.

The entrepreneur will feel as though he/she was here eons ago but, in reality, just a few years have passed. There is also a feeling of pressure about the many people who depend on good decisions and consistent follow-through.

Scar Tissue Event Twenty-One: Controlling the Ego

"Look at what I have accomplished!"

It can be hard for many to share credit; after all it was the entrepreneur's idea to start with, wasn't it? A look at the seven previously listed ways in which smart people can falter reveals that just about all of them are related directly or indirectly to a misapplied ego.

Directly related to misapplied ego is arrogance. When ego and arrogance are combined it will become nearly impossible to complete the saga of successful entrepreneurial development. As the old adage teaches, "Pride always goes before the fall."

I cannot think of one hugely successful entrepreneurial event that did not include other people. Success is not created in a vacuum. Value simply cannot be created without the help of others. At this point judgment, particularly good judgment, is becoming more and more important for both entrepreneur and venture.

The entrepreneur's ability as leader to successfully transform an idea and create an organization that will have a life of its own really comes down to making the right calls at the right times. This may the most important job of being an effective entrepreneur. It is easy to assume that good judgment is the result of extensive experience. Experience is an essential component but we all know brilliant people with extensive experience who consistently make bad judgment calls.

So how can the entrepreneur assure greater success through making good judgment calls? Warren Bennis and Noel Tichy (both highly regarded as leadership consultants, teachers and authors) have together written a new book titled, Judgment and Leadership, How Winning Leaders Make Great Calls, (Penguin Group, 2007). This work explains the process of successful judgment and is one I highly recommend.

In short summary, the authors address the dimensions in which the process takes place:

· Time: Recognizing the signs that a decision is necessary and then the follow through on execution.

· Domain: Three dimensions in which most important calls are centered; people, strategy and crisis.

· Constituencies: Informing all who are impacted, considering interests and managing relationships. The authors add that four types of knowledge are needed to navigate the waters of good judgment: self-knowledge, social networking knowledge, organizational knowledge and contextual knowledge (all the other stakeholders).

Long-term success is totally dependent on being able to make good judgment calls. An entrepreneur should be able to recognize the critical crossroads in his/her company and then gather the information necessary to make an informed decision. Then communicate that decision throughout the impacted constituencies, align them and gain support for implementation. A quote to remember from the authors: "Making judgment calls is the essential job of a leader. With good judgment, little else matters. Without good judgment, nothing else matters."

Good Judgment/Bad Judgment

In the early days of Medtronic, the founder Earl Bakken, reached a critical crossroad. He understood his personal skill set as well as his personal interests. It was at this point that a young Minneapolis attorney named Tom Holloran, who had helped Medtronic with its incorporation three years earlier, became a board member. Holloran was influential in assisting in the early development of the company, moving into various posts in addition to his board seat. Eventually, Holloran became president of the company. Had the inventor/scientist, Bakken, not allowed this transition, the odds are that Medtronic, as we know it, may never have come to be.

While Medtronic offers an example of good judgment, online marketplace eBay's choices have not been as positive.

An Oct. 27, 2008 article in Forbes Magazine, "Too Smart for Its Own Good," tells the succession (and progression) story of eBay from its founders to professional management team. Here, the early mantra of "Don't screw it up" has been forgotten. Most of the new succession management came from the professional management consulting industry, which, like many who are good at telling others how to do things, somehow have difficulty when they own the responsibility of execution. The company, according to the article, has become data driven with decisions by committee. A former executive said that people who do not use eBay now run the company. In the early days, employees would announce how many items they had bought and sold on the site. The culture has definitely changed and not for the better.

When management is arrogant enough to believe they have the answers and that input from the bottom up needs to be filtered through multiple layers of rules and bureaucracy, generally a company will find itself on the road to failure.

Obviously, Earl Bakken recognized his management skill limitations and, through listening to wise counsel, sought another person with skills he lacked. He was able to use good judgment along with excellent people selection to see his company become the great one it is today.

In the case of eBay, the founder has stepped far enough away that the culture that led to early success has not been maintained. Key people have left in disgust and top-down management has been put in place.

Earlier, I said that at this critical stage the role of the owner/CEO has to become one of the "keeper of the culture" and vision of the company to assure its continued success. The two examples discussed in this section point to the importance of keeping the culture of an organization viable. eBay is now being called the "IBM of Silicon Valley," choked by rules and bureaucracy. This is the last thing I would wish on any entrepreneurial success.

Conversely, Bakken, even into his retirement, would bring patients who were alive because of a medical device the company made to company meetings so that employees could see the good that was accomplished. This went a long way to reinforce the vision of this medical products company.

Scar Tissue Event Twenty-Two: Failure to Grow

"Why do I need growth, won't that just add more issues?"

Growth is nearly always an issue that comes up at this stage of development.

Usually, the early rush of sales growth has started to ease but competition is becoming a bigger factor. There is always the temptation to stay small and profitable and to try and etch out a sustainable niche. Growth certainly brings with it additional issues to be addressed. However, when managing a company, one must remember that change is constant while growth can be optional.

If the venture did not get its start with O.P.M. (other people's money), this is an option but one that needs to be given careful thought. However, if outside money was raised and growth has been enough to build a great team of people who are there for long-term employment with personal development and advancement opportunity, there is little choice but to grow.

I recently received a phone call from a business friend who runs a small manufacturing firm. He was a little dismayed because he had just analyzed his sales by product category and discovered one of his key products significantly slid. He said he had the feeling that this was about to happen and failed to take early action. Mainly, he said, because he knew that the life cycle on this product had peaked and he knew of no way to combat the inevitable. He felt a little desperate to find new product ideas but did not know how to go about it.

As I thought about what he had told me, I knew that I also have struggled in the past trying to constantly "reinvent" a product, a service or maybe even a basic business concept in order to inject some new life into a maturing situation. Ideas are not always easy to come by and it is especially hard when going it alone.

My guess is that many with sole proprietorships might now be thinking, "Okay, so where do I go for help with ideas?" There are many avenues to travel for new business offerings, enhancements, and added value. A few suggestions follow:

Customers

Chris Berghoff, a good friend who owns Control Products, Inc., never seems to lack for good ideas. His company makes some proprietary electronic control products and also does some custom work for original equipment manufacturer (OEM). When I asked Berghoff how he constantly came up with new ideas, he told me that one of his strategies was to occasionally go out and visit with customers. He would ask them what they were doing that was new to gauge new opportunity for his company. He also would ask if there were improvements or modifications needed on products already being sold to this customer.

Besides being a great way to build rapport and diffuse problems, Berghoff said he always came back from these road trips with at least one or two new product ideas or product enhancements. Considering this once little company has grown 10-fold over a relatively short period of time, this might be an idea for all to emulate. While interviewing a customer, it is also important to ask if they have ever considered anyone else for this product/service and what might cause them to switch suppliers. This may aid in discovery of an added-value service that can further cement the relationship.

Employees

Employee ideas/suggestions should be followed up and followed through, not simply ignored. Invariably in speaking with employees of business people, who claim to never receive any employee ideas, I am told over and over again that "management" ignores and fails to respond to their ideas. So, tragically ideas dry up and young employees, feeling that they are not listened to or appreciated, seek employment elsewhere. Every business could use young, enthusiastic, creative people. Simple listening and following through will help young talent stay enthused and committed to the business.

A small reward system for ideas is a simple encouragement technique. In the past, I have seen business people who are good at this use anything from $1 to $5 for just a suggestion. The key is for the manager to then follow through on each and every one. If an idea is turned down, then an explanation of why is in order. If accepted, then some assessment of value has to be placed on the idea/suggestion.

Compensation can be a flat amount, a percentage of savings/revenue or some combination of the two. I have seen companies use anything from $250 to several thousand dollars as a flat reward and others use 25 to 40 percent of expense savings or 2 to 5 percent of sales of a new revenue idea. Financial incentives should be structured realistically for each individual business. It also is important to recognize that ideas that may not be really great are, nevertheless, worth applying. A smaller prize, like $25, can be awarded for any idea that may not be significant but is worthwhile.

Suppliers

Spending time with suppliers, much like Berghoff does with his customers is always worthwhile. Here is an opportunity to seek out ideas and gain insight into industry trends. Most are willing to assist - even discussing what the competition is doing - to preserve a good customer relationship. Using this tactic many years ago, I was able to find out that a key competitor was for sale and later successfully made the acquisition.

Industry

This is an old methodology but an important one. Voracious reading and visiting trade shows and conventions will help an owner/CEO stay up to date on industry trends. Talking with other non-competitors also can be an enormous source of good ideas and reveal new opportunities.

Like many, when I first started in business, I could not afford to make many mistakes. To help me with this, I gathered a group of similarly-sized business owners in my industry. None of us competed directly. We would meet quarterly to compare financial statements and talk about what each of us was doing to add new business. When new ideas came up, each member would take turns trying it out. Then, we would all adopt what worked, limiting the risk and the cost of implementation. This consortium led to all of us joining together to start a related business, so we could diversify, a business that grew into a multi-million dollar concern.

Resources on Growth/Added Value

Jim Champy has written a book titled, OUTSMART! (Pearson Education, Inc., 2008), which deals with strategies for sustainable success. Champy is the chairman of Perot Systems' consulting practice and is perhaps best known for his book titled, Reengineering the Corporation. He writes about outsmarting the competition with greater flexibility and adaptability.

Champy suggests tactics like looking for the hidden niches where the competition isn't and making sure that service levels remain excellent. Delivering products and/or services that are not being done by others, perhaps extended hours or after hours availability, is another strategy.

Likely, there are areas where things could be done better. Inquiry may reveal a standard, long-standing industry practice that exists for the convenience of the industry, not the customer. For example, the Sunday closing practice in the retail automobile industry can make it difficult for the dual income family to find the time to purchase a car. The concept is to, as Champy says, "widen your lens, but narrow your focus." Opportunity may exist for a different application of an existing product.

Two other books speak directly to this issue: The Granularity of Growth by Patrick Viguerie, Sven Smit and Mehrdad Baghai (John Wiley & Sons, Inc. 2008) and The Momentum Effect by J.C. Larreche (Wharton School Publishing, 2008). The first book's authors are McKinsey consultants. A graduate business school professor writes the second book from INSEAD, in France (one of the world's largest business schools). Both books deal in large part with the importance of added value creation to continue to foster future growth. Both books also highlight the importance of growth in order to survive in today's economy. In the first book the authors quote studies that have shown that higher growth companies have a survival rate that is five to six times greater than low growth ones.

The Granularity of Growth authors point out that

one of the key decisions about growth is where to compete. One of the obvious choices here is making sure the market segment is experiencing broad customer acceptance, demand and rapid growth itself. Other choices relate to specific geographic areas and deciding which new markets to enter.

Viguerie, Smit and Baghai define three horizons for sustained and profitable growth. These are: 1) Extending and defending initial core business, 2) Building and developing new emerging business and 3) Creating viable options. In the first horizon, the entrepreneur will need to pursue excellence in execution and watch to move the business into markets with the greatest opportunity for continued growth. In the second, new product niches in new markets and acquisitions to aid growth will be focal points. Finally in the third, the organization diversifies into entirely new product lines and market areas through new product development and/or acquisitions. The entrepreneur will by now most likely have a portfolio of products, which need to be managed, much like a garden. Promoting products are nurtured while less promising ones are weeded out.

In The Momentum Effect (Wharton School Publishing, 2008) the focus is on creating and sustaining momentum to foster growth. Author Jean Claude Larreche stresses the importance of "delighted" customers. That is, customers who are so satisfied and excited about their purchase transaction that they will tell others. Larreche stresses that in order to do this, effort must be put into discovering the sources of dissatisfaction and then seeing that improvement takes place A.S.A.P. Customers must be listened to carefully and then every complaint is followed up until the customer is satisfied. I always told anyone who interfaced with the customer that we had three policies when it came to handling complaints: 1) Satisfy the customer, 2) Satisfy the customer and 3) Satisfy the customer. A dissatisfied customer can be converted when compensated beyond their expectations and, in the process, that customer will be even more loyal than before.

I have an example of customer conversion from my own experience. When I was in the supermarket business, we sold about 5,000 turkeys each Thanksgiving holiday with no complaints. One particular Thanksgiving, a store manager received a call from an irate customer that the turkey she had just taken out of the oven was so tough you could not cut it with a knife. She said she would never come back to our store and was so angry that she would not leave her name or phone number.

Since that store had caller I.D., the manager obtained her name. He got together with the deli manager and, since we baked full turkey dinners for customers, boxed up one of our turkeys with all the trimmings and took it to her house. She was surprised to see him at the door and even more surprised to see that he brought a complete dinner. Needless to say, she remained a loyal customer forever. (Years later she admitted to the manager that she had been in a hurry and probably overcooked the bird.)

This story leads in to another aspect of momentum that Larreche talks about - retention. If possible, he advises tracking lost customers over retained ones each year. The goal is a 90 percent retention rate. Anything below 70 percent indicates the average customer lifetime is insignificant.

Scar Tissue Event Twenty-Three: Failure to carefully monitor customer service

"Once the sale has been made I shouldn't have to worry!"

As previously noted, in order to grow successfully, perhaps, the most important ingredient is creating a cadre of extremely satisfied customers. Even those who have chosen to control or limit growth will still need to have happy customers. Remember, one needs to think carefully about choosing a path of limited growth. The reasons for this are two-fold:

· If a product/service has been created that is in high demand and through limitation of growth, customers are turned away, pent-up demand for the product/service will naturally attract competition into the market. If competitors are more efficient or can execute better, sales can be lost.

· Unfortunately, fixed expenses aren't fixed. Costs like taxes, insurance, utilities, rent, etc. have a habit of creeping upwards. This will eventually begin to eat into margins and erode profits. Sales growth can offset expense and prevent the constant rising of prices.

Careful consideration should be given to growth or no growth options. Either way, the customer transaction must be monitored to ensure survival.

Patricia Seybold, a consultant in this area and also author of a best seller titled Customers.com, wrote a first book titled The Customer Revolution (Crown Publishing, 2001). In it she describes the three principles driving the "revolution." These are:

· Customers are in control

· Customer relationships count

· Customer experiences with a product/service do matter.

In an information society, people know more and as a result demand more. Remember, those not satisfied only need to look to the Internet, where in most cases they are able to easily find competitive products and services no matter where they might live.

So, what steps are needed to ensure a satisfied customer?

The first step is to find out everything possible about the customer through maintaining some key measurements such as the total number of customers, the average sale to each, who and what they are (try to get a handle on demographic profile), satisfaction level with product/service, gauge interest in other unavailable products, and, the hardest of all, measure yearly turnover in customers. This last measure will help gauge customer loyalty.

Naturally, gathering and maintaining customer data can be time consuming and onerous if done by hand but fortunately there is software available that can support the effort. In fact, this whole area of customer service management has a term today, it is called Customer Relationship Management or CRM. There are numerous websites to help you begin such a program. Three I would recommend are: www.crm-forum.com, www.crmba.com/ and www.2crm.com/. The first helps with understanding of various methodologies, the second helps find industry benchmarks to measure against and the third evaluates available software by business size and industry.

Expert Advice on Customer Service

Seybold urges focus on the total customer experience. This means consistent representation of the company in all communication and customer contact followed by flawless execution. Customers are loyal to their experience with a product/service not to the product/service itself. I am certain that those who give thought to a particular brand would conclude that their loyalty is an outgrowth of satisfaction with the brand and/or service. Customers will make the switch if a new brand delivers better service. Therefore, the company/brand is not as important as the experience.

So, what can one do to build strong customer relationships and the resulting loyal customer base? Seybold suggests several steps.

A product or service first must be differentiated from the competition - something that others don't do that customers value enough to help sway their purchase decision.

Once unique product characteristics have been identified, the entrepreneur must develop a passion for his/her customers that everyone associated with the organization can clearly see and understand. This means demonstrating concern about customers' experiences with the company and the resulting outcome. An organization and its associates must value a customer's time, craft business hours for their convenience and deliver a seamless customer experience. Customers today want a hassle-free, convenient, and consistent purchase experience.

Along with developing and demonstrating passion for the customer, the owner/CEO should look at two additional factors. First, through the metrics that the company has developed, the owner should try to completely understand what matters most to customers when they make a purchase. Then, ensure that this is delivered each and every time - measure to be sure. Finally, supportive operations should run efficiently and do everything possible to assist in making the customer's experience satisfactory.

From personal experience, I know that any owner/CEO who begins to focus on the customer and the customer experience with his/her business will soon recognize customers that have left and not come back. Another component to a customer service program should be to develop strategies and tactics to win them back. Although winning back a lost customer may seem costly, it is usually more cost-effective to regain a lost customer back than to win a new one.

The book, SATISFACTION, (Portfolio of Penguin Group, 2007), by Chris Denove and James D. Power (of J.D. Power and Associates) reinforces the above mentioned by writing about how every great company listens to the voice of the customer. Since J.D. Power and Associates is famous for product quality and customer satisfaction surveys since 1968, paying attention to what they have to say seems in order.

Denove and Power stress that there is a direct relationship between business growth and success and customer satisfaction. They assert that every customer comes with some sort of expectation as a result of word-of-mouth or an advertising or marketing piece. Matching those expectations with the actual experience is what's important. Customer expectations are never static, they constantly move upward. Therefore, there is a corresponding need to continually address improving customer interactions. Many businesses tend to focus on things that may not mean much to the customer while ignoring smaller things that are really causing a disservice. The way to find this out is to simply ask.

Fred Reichheld, the author of The Ultimate Question, (HBR Publishing, 2006), says regular customer surveys of customers need to be given. The questions to ask are simple: "Would you recommend us to a friend?" and "Why or why not?"

SATISFACTION, authors address the different methods which should be used for different types of businesses to really get an idea how each needs to address customer satisfaction. The sectors on which the authors focus are service providers, product manufacturers, and retailers.

Service providers need to address the difference between the tangible quality of the service provided and the satisfaction with how service was provided. Many service companies have excellent technical skills but may be lacking in the manner with which those skills are delivered. A couple of recognizable examples are the skillful surgeon who has a terrible bedside manner or the top-notch plumber who never shows up on time.

Product manufacturers have two primary touch points, execution and quality. Both separate and distinct; execution pertains to design, features and performance, while quality refers to how the product lasts and functions. There can be two secondary touch-points for manufacturers, sales and service experience.

Retail businesses have four factors to consider: location, availability, price and shopping experience. Denove and Power say the shopping experience can be a major deciding factor and the ambiance of location, interpersonal experience, and store policies (returns, exchanges, hours, etc.) all play a role. To those factors, I would add another - flexibility of policies. A retailer adept at customer service will know when an exception should be made.

Once established, customer service policies are only effective if those associates who interface directly with the customer follow through. As I mentioned earlier, my No. 1 customer service policy is to "satisfy the customer." Of course the key to making this work is trusting associates to do the right thing. This also means empowerment - allowing associates to have flexibility and choice about how the customer receives satisfaction.

Many owners fear such employee empowerment. They believe it will result in an associate "giving away the store." It has been my experience that this isn't the case. And, the quicker the complaint is satisfied, the greater the customer satisfaction. It is much easier to build a business around satisfied customers, who keep coming back and bringing new customers with them.

One last factor that must be in place to build a successful customer satisfaction program is hiring the right people. Any venture needs people who actually like serving people. First impressions are important and customers will be forming an impression of an organization within the first few seconds of contact with an associate.

What kind of first impression does a potential associate give in the interview process? Personality can be more important than technical skills. It is easier to teach technical skills than change personality traits - it's certainly easier to teach someone with a pleasant personality. An owner needs to be willing to pay above average wages to people who fit these criteria. This, in itself, will help attract like-minded people. Also, look at the company benefits package. Dynamic people with pleasing personalities usually have their choice of where to work. An attractive benefits package and work environment are key to luring quality employees. The rewards of greater sales and profitability will make it worthwhile.

I stated earlier that the cost of regaining a customer, in most cases, is less than obtaining a new one. The reason for this is that these customers already know the product line/service, the entrepreneur knows them, and hopefully understands why they left. To begin to address the issues that caused them to leave in the first place should not be excessively costly. Of course, this means a direct personal contact from someone. I would recommend that someone be the owner/CEO, to verify the reason they have ceased to buy. An argumentative approach should not be taken - listen carefully and sympathize with their issues. Accept responsibility for whatever happened and offer a generous solution. Remember the value of long-term, solid customer relationships.

A book written by Jill Griffin and Michael Lowenstein titled: Customer Winback (Jossey-Bass, Inc. 2001) helps immensely in discovering the ways and means to gain back lost customers. Both Griffin and Lowenstein are independent consultants in the field of customer retention and customer loyalty.

Griffin and Lowenstein suggest offering customer options if all lost business cannot be won back at once - a partial restoration will allow the business to concentrate on reestablishing trust. Once the reason for the defection is discovered, a solution should then be developed so that it does not happen again and report that solution back to the customer. This also will work for at-risk customers who are unhappy and may be considering leaving.

The authors suggest that at any time as many as one-third of customers may be considering defecting to the competition. Generally, customers will not come to the CEO/owner and complain, but they will tell others. The entire staff must be customer-sensitive to complaints and report them to the appropriate person for follow-up. Basically, the entrepreneur must make it as easy as possible for someone to complain, and then gain a reputation for quick follow-up and resolution.

In one of my businesses, I had a customer complaint form that I would have the contact person fill out. I would insist that the person initially contacted by the customer handle complaints immediately. I gave each staff person wide latitude in resolving customer issues, remembering always our three customer satisfaction policies. All of these forms would cross my desk and I would follow-up with phone calls to make certain that the customer had been satisfied. I also took this time to assure the customer that the issue that caused the complaint had been handled and that it would not happen again.

Griffin and Lowenstein also mention Noriako Kano of the Science University of Tokyo. Kano has suggested three levels of customer satisfaction: basic, expected and unanticipated. Kano claims that most companies perform the first two fairly well but it takes execution at the third level to begin to build strong customer loyalty.

All of the expert advice above points clearly

in the same direction: Handle customers well and effectively deal with the issues of complaints and customer interaction. This is the only way to reach the holy grail of customer service, which many call "stickiness."

I have worked with many businesses, which sought help in finding new customers. These companies are usually looking for new ways to advertise and market to bring in new customers. My first question to these people is: "What happened to those who left?" If an organization is ineffective at retaining customers then the best marketing and advertising in the world will do nothing to make up for this deficiency.

At times, I have seen businesses that give more than acceptable customer service still have issues with retention. I believe this often stems from naively ignoring the established base because of the awareness that service is satisfactory. Yet time and time again, when turnover is measured these same companies are completely surprised by the amount they have. Some will even have less than "industry norms" and others maybe around the norm but still it will be less than acceptable to astute management.

Why does this occur? At times, a concentrated effort on outstanding customer service can lead to complacency and customers fall through the cracks. For example, businesses need to carefully consider the impact that offering an outlandishly low price to new customers only will have on the established customer base.

When a business is enjoying a high customer satisfaction rating it is building a cadre of loyal customers. However, it is easy to begin to slip on the little things that first brought those customers when focus shifts to further expansion of the total customer base. The average sale per customer is likely the first place erosion will show up. Loyal customers, as long as the service level is being maintained, will not quit completely. They will, if they feel unappreciated, begin to spread their purchases out more to other suppliers. Measuring this customer "slippage" will offer a solid, recognizable and early indicator that also will allow early remedy to the situation.

Gauging Customer Satisfaction

An easy way to begin to prevent slippage of the established customer base is to begin with a simple question: "How easy is it for any customer to do business with this company?"

Here are tips from other successful business people that can help with this issue:

An owner can call his/her own place of business disguised as a customer to gain a sense of how associates deal with customers. Much can be learned from this simple approach. A hired "secret" shopper is a similar tactic that can be helpful.

The process for handling complaints should be easily accessed and resolved efficiently without question. Make sure loyal customers are recognized and corrective action is followed through A.S.A.P. I recently made a purchase in a large sporting goods retailer and when I reviewed the cash register tape it had written on the bottom: "Hi, I am Joe Smith and I am the manager of this store. My direct telephone number is 900----- and I want you to call me if you have any questions or problems with your purchase." This is an impressive way to tell customers that management cares about their satisfaction. (Of course Joe needs to be there when I call or this tactic will work against him and his company.)

Many businesses make the false assumption that the established customer base understands everything about their offerings. So, less effort is made to acquaint established customers with changes than would be made with a new customer. Continuous training of all personnel must be provided so that they can handle the majority, if not all, of the questions that a customer might ask. It also is particularly important to keep a continuous open line of communication with the established base. They should feel like an insider to new offerings. This is absolutely essential.

Make sure that parking is always available and free if at all possible. One firm that had many established customers returning on a regular had reserved parking right up front for them.

Convenience and accessibility is essential and even more so for the loyal customer. They should feel special. For the professional firm, that means access, many times, during off hours. A friend of mine who was a professional accountant always had his home telephone number on his business card. He said that his small business clients often needed answers to questions during times he was not in his office.

There are some additional the things that also can help in the quest to attain high satisfaction rates and foster customer retention. Again, some of these suggestions may not fit every circumstance but I would guess that everyone could find something here that is applicable to their business.

Work with employees to remember customer names. There is nothing that makes someone feel better than when a place of business remembers his or her name.

When a new customer makes a purchase, many businesses will follow-up with a note or card of thanks. Established business should be recognized for continued loyalty as well. When out of town recently I had a minor problem with my car. I stopped at a dealership, which is a competitor to the one where I purchased my car. This competitor followed-up with a box of chocolates delivered to my home and asked me to consider doing business with them. My previous dealership always acted like it was an inconvenience to service my car. (Notice I said "previous.")

Small gestures can create loyalty. I own two cars and do business with yet another dealership for my second car. Since I travel quite a bit, I had arranged to drop off my car with this dealer for some work while I was away. I told the service manager when I would return and he said he would try to have the car ready. The evening of my return, at 7 p.m., I received a call from the service manager saying my car was ready for pickup the next day. He did not have to do that, but that small gesture cemented me as a customer. In addition, the car was fixed right and the work was done on time.

An extra effort always is appreciated. My daughter has three children and most readers can appreciate how hectic this can be, especially when one of them is ill. This happened recently and she told me that her local druggist arranged for a prescription to be delivered. Her local car dealer also helped out, by picking up her car, servicing it, and then returning it. Large corporate competitors won't usually add "extra touches" but they do reward loyalty and cement retention.

I am sure that with a little thought, many more ways to provide the extra touches that go into developing high customer satisfaction and the resulting high customer retention rates could be devised. An entrepreneur must look at what other successful businesses in the industry do and then copy successful ideas. Those who spend extra effort on ways to retain customers will be spending a lot less time, money and effort trying to figure out how to market to new ones.

Section Five: Finally Maturity, Separation and Legacy

"Goodwill is the one and only asset that competition cannot undersell nor destroy."
Marshall Field

Chapter Eight

"What does it mean to have an enduring company?"
"This sounds like it will cost money"

Much has been written lately about the need to re-address ethics in business. Some of the commentary has focused on the need for business schools to do a better job of teaching the subject. It would seem that it would be a subject that needs to be addressed and discussed in that forum. However, since ethics are so enmeshed with one's value system and values are difficult if not impossible to change, instruction may need to begin much sooner in life. I do not propose a solution for this dilemma outside of, hopefully, provoking some further thought.

First, I should admit an upfront bias - I can see no justifiable reason to operate an entrepreneurial endeavor with anything less than the utmost ethical principles.

With this in mind, let me offer a traditional approach to ethics with my added personal caveats to enhance this guideline. Traditionally, decisions with ethical implications were weighed with two measurements in mind: First, is it legal? Secondly, are the consequences bad? To this I would add the following: Is it balanced? Does it take into account all stakeholders? Is it fair in both the short term and long term? Will it promote a win/win? Does it show responsibility to others? Finally, how will I feel about myself?

Close examination of truly successful enduring companies will reveal that most were founded on very strong ethical principles. Generally, the founder was not shy about communicating the values that he/she felt to be critical to them personally and to the company.

Earlier, I referenced James Heskett and John Kotter of Harvard and their five-year study, which compared companies with open management systems to those with traditional, hierarchical systems. The study measured four criteria: sales growth, employment growth, profits growth and business value growth.

Recall that revenue growth in the open companies was four times greater, employment growth eight times greater, profitability growth more than 700 times greater and company value growth was 12 times greater. This provides compelling evidence that companies run this way fare significantly better in key measurements of business success. True openness will help maintain ethical principles.

Given that high ethical standards can lead to greater business success, the question that naturally follows then is: How is such a culture created? I recommend a small book, Managing by Values (Berrett-Kohler Publishers, 1997) by Ken Blanchard and Michael O'Conner. This work provides great insight into this whole matter of ethical management.

Although a book can be a starting point for formulating ideas about ethics in business, ultimately, the entrepreneur must make many of those judgment calls on his/her own. When instructing people who are just starting a business, I strongly suggest that they begin their business plan with a set of values that outlines who they are and what they wish the company to stand for. This, then, becomes part of the company vision statement.

Once values are established, it is imperative, as mentioned earlier, that the people selected as associates share those values. In the January 28,

2003 edition of Wall Street Journal there was an excellent article that described how the new CEO of Mattel goes about assuring himself that values are shared during the interview process. He focuses on the candidate's life experiences and has general discussions about the individual's values. He spends little time on the resume itself. He said, "I try to understand their values, what is most important to them and whether they will fit here."

Vision has been overplayed in some ways yet I know of no other way that a founder can effectively communicate just what it is that he/she hopes this entity will reflect in terms of ethical values. When strong vision is combined with effective communication, the result is an organization with a shared purpose. This helps build strong ethical cultures and successful companies. Beyond Entrepreneurship: Turning Your Business Into An Enduring Great Company by James Collins (Prentice-Hall, 1992) offers greater insight.

Scar Tissue Event Twenty-four: Failure to Build Community Relations

"I thought providing jobs was enough."

Failure to build community relations may not result in organizational failure, but must be a part of the total company package if there is desire to create an enduring company. It makes little difference whether the company is a local consumer-based entity like a retailer, a manufacturer or a service-based business it is still a part of the community in which it is based.

Like it or not, this means that company and its owner(s) do owe something beyond paying taxes and providing jobs. If an entrepreneur has built a great company based on well-articulated values, then community service should be a part of the overall vision.

Company programs designed to benefit the greater community are also an important ingredient in an effective marketing plan. These programs, when designed well, not only benefit the community but also can go a long way toward fostering a long-lasting relationship that will pay dividends in the future. It is important to treat that relationship with broader stakeholders as a franchise. It is also important to continue to foster that relationship in order to earn trust that brings with it customer loyalty.

Most everyone in Minnesota can remember when the former Dayton Hudson Company was under attack by a corporate raider and how the entire state, including the Legislature, rallied to help fend off this attempted acquisition. That widespread support was fostered by years of community activity, support, and involvement by the company. This is the kind of community "franchise" that I would urge any business to work at developing. It is definitely a win/win for both company and community. In most cases the cost of such a program is much less than many other forms of marketing and it can become, as in the Dayton case, a formidable competitive advantage.

I am sure at this point most readers are questioning how fair it is to compare a large corporation's philanthropic community activity with what a small company can do. I will acknowledge that gifts of largesse from a large corporation do make headlines but the small company owner can create something that is just as effective for far less cost. Customers and employees alike appreciate and care about the reputation of the company they work for and do business with.

Where should this effort begin? It is important, especially in a small company, to design a program that fits with company image and one that can meet both a community and business objective. A small company cannot do it all; therefore, it is important to determine what will have the greatest impact. It is more important to use a selective approach rather than a scattergun. This will lead to greater effectiveness and recognition as a leader in a philanthropic area.

Begin by talking to employees to find out where they might be spending their volunteer time. Sometimes, support can be offered by giving extra time off to employees to assist with special events. Setting up a small matching grant program will boost the impact of their private financial contributions. Cost control can be achieved through an annual dollar limitation and/or by the limiting the number of organizations.

Examination of the current business strategy and where there is desire to strengthen ties to certain community groups, thereby, broadening the customer base, should take place next. Partnering with other non-profit organizations will bolster impact.

Following are examples from small businesses, which might spur ideas:

A small restaurant chain supports the arts community by seeking out local struggling artists and purchasing their works to be incorporated into the décor of its new restaurant.

A small drug retailer formed a small charitable fund and tied it to the county social services director. Whenever this director saw a need unfulfilled, she was able to tap this fund. No cash was exchanged but instead gift certificates were purchased to fill specific needs of clients.

A small town bank established a $2,500 annual scholarship program at the local high school for a college-bound student with the most need.

A very creative Phil Romano, founder of Fuddruckers, once owned a small Italian restaurant called Macaroni's. Monday and Tuesday nights were slow so once a month on a randomly selected Monday or Tuesday all patrons got their meals free. This built tremendous goodwill and helped build two slow evenings. Although not a direct community relation program it did build tremendous community recognition.

Every Tuesday a locally-owned supermarket offered 5 percent discounts to senior citizens.

A newly established home developer partnered with the local Ronald McDonald House and had one of his homes on the Parade of Homes named as the Ronald McDonald Charity Event. The interior decorator that furnished the house sold the interior accessories at a discount. The difference from the purchases was donated to the charity.

A local car dealer had a chipping green installed in the backyard. For a $5 donation people were allowed to attempt a hole-in-one and the chance to win a new car. Needless to say, this attracted a lot of publicity for the new company.

At Erdman's Supermarkets, we told church parishioners (and our customers) in our community to save their receipts and turn them into the church. We then would reimburse the church 1/2 percent of the total. Twenty-seven churches agreed to participate. In addition, our company put another 1/2 percent into a trust that would give purchase credits to the impoverished and homeless for staples. During the 30-plus years we have run this program, more than $533,000 has flowed back into the community.

These examples illustrate the importance of looking at the community as a partner in business. Owners can find creative ways to "give back" that serve both business and the community. This effort will reward both well in the long run.

The Entrepreneur at a Crossroad

Building an enduring company takes time and a focused effort. Having successfully managed through all the transitions previously discussed, the owner may now find him/herself questioning if it's as much fun as it was in the beginning. Next, comes the question (and decision) of whether the entrepreneur should stay involved with the entity that he/she has created.

Most readers will have probably heard the entrepreneurial success story about Tom's of Maine.

The company founded by Tom Chappell sells natural personal care products; the product most recognizable is toothpaste.

In a story published in the October 1989 issue of Inc Magazine, Chappell shared that the process of becoming more professionalized left him feeling somewhat alienated from his own company. He considered selling.

Chappell felt that many of the new people he had hired did not share his ethics or values. However, selling would leave him with basically nothing to do and he was too young to retire. He chose to go back to school on a part-time basis. He went to Harvard Divinity School where he was able to better grasp his own personal values and the values that he wished to be reflected in his company. He believed that to be complete, his company needed to better connect with the community and its customer base through the values the company portrayed.

"The quest simply for more of anything is inherently unsatisfying. If there is no point or joy in what you are doing, or if you lose sight of the point, then just measuring your progress can't make it worthwhile or fun," Chappell says. "What drives and organizes people are values, not strategy or quantitative rewards; if I can organize people around purpose that is the most powerful form of leadership."

Ichak Adizes wrote a book 20 years ago that went a long way to helping the entrepreneur better understand how to manage his company through the many growth transitions that occur. The title of the book is, Corporate Lifecycles: How and Why Corporations Grow and Die and What to Do About It (Prentice-Hall, 1988). The book is still available and applicable. In it he describes the lifecycles that companies go through using the same analogy of the growth of a child.

However, Adizes believes that, unlike a human organism, business organizations do not have to grow old and die. Flexibility and control, when correctly applied, are key. In the early days, companies tend to be unbalanced with more flexibility than control. As they move through the development cycle, controls are added and the pendulum swings in the other direction. The objective, says the author, is to make sure that a relative balance of each remains throughout the growth cycle to better enhance the staying power of the company.

Some of the above mentioned principles are described in the book, George Washington on Leadership by Richard Brookhiser, (Basic Books, 2008). According to Brookhiser, General Washington ran two start-ups, the American Army and the presidency as well as chairing the most important meeting in United States history, the Constitutional Convention.

Washington had setbacks, including failure when he was defeated early on in the French and Indian War at Fort Necessity. Yet, he was greatly respected, even revered, as the founding CEO of a new nation. The key, says the author, was his management style.

Brookhiser asserts that Washington had an ability to learn from failure and modestly acknowledge the need for self-improvement instead of blaming others. Washington looked to the Roman philosopher, Seneca, to learn how to behave while under stress in a leadership role. He shunned flashy rhetoric and used simple and direct words. Through this approach, he moved men to re-enlist, mutineers to return to duty and moved his officers to tears at war's end. Washington generally maintained a tolerant view of his subordinates' failures, idiosyncrasies and weaknesses. He worked with all to enhance their strengths instead, lessons that all of us can learn from today.

Long-term success ensures an enduring company. To accomplish this will require following management principles laid out earlier. These principles, when applied and integrated over time will help the entrepreneur transition successfully as various lifecycle hurdles present themselves.

Another book, this one by Karl Albrecht, titled, The Power of Minds at Work (AMACON, 2002) deals with the flipside, or organizational dysfunction and the impact it can have on long-term viability. The author asserts that too many companies waste the collective intelligence and talents of their employees. Most of these are the same companies that will claim that "people make the difference" but in the majority of these cases the saying is only a mindless platitude.

Albrecht says the leaders of these companies read about how today's organizations have grown too large and impersonal and feel that by adopting a "slogan" that they have effectively dealt with the problem. He speaks about the power of collective intelligence in an organization. This concept is compared to collective stupidity with a focus on how effective organizations can become when the former is achieved. Albrecht defines different types of organizational intelligence, which he calls the seven dimensions.

Strategic Vision

People need to know why this organization was created and where it might be headed in the future. Why should they devote a part of their life to helping the entrepreneur achieve whatever it is he/she wishes to achieve?

Shared Fate

Everyone likes to work for a common purpose. Some have called this "the common enemy." Something that rallies the troops around the flag. People need to understand how they are valued and how they fit into the grand scheme of things. How does their role affect the success of the organization?

Appetite for Change

Every organization needs change to present new and exciting challenges to those who are part of it. New opportunities allow growth and learning.

Heart

Good leadership will inspire people to reach seemingly unattainable goals, to give over and above. I define this as part of the entrepreneurial leader's work contract.

Alignment and Congruence

Everything within an organization needs to be aligned toward the common purpose (goal). That means that processes, systems, policies, reward systems, structure, etc. should all lead people in the direction of helping the organization to succeed.

Knowledge Deployment

Sharing knowledge, data and information openly in an organization is the only way to ever develop collective intelligence.

Performance Pressure

When an entrepreneur is successful at the first six dimensions people "buy in" to the organization to such an extent that performance pressure comes from within and not from the top.

For many entrepreneurs whom I have come to know and appreciate, there are occasions to ponder the measure of one's success. Reflection on goals at the outset is in order here. Back at the start, what were the goals? Have those goals been accomplished? Remember to seek meaning and purpose first and success will follow. Those able to achieve goals with integrity still intact have surely been successful.

I have always found that Ralph Waldo Emerson best defined success, at least for me:

> To laugh often and much;
> To win the respect of intelligent people
> and the affection of children;
> To earn the appreciation of honest
> critics and endure the betrayal of false
> friends;

To appreciate beauty;
To find the best in others;
To leave the world a bit better, whether
by a healthy child, a garden patch or a
redeemed social condition;
To know even one life has breathed
easier because you have lived;
This is to have succeeded.

Chapter Nine

"Life is a journey, entrepreneurship is a passion. Creating your own firm is a passionate journey."
-Unknown

Parting Company and Moving On

"Is it necessary for me to leave?"

Throughout this book, I have attempted to help the reader recognize that organizations move through developmental phases as they grow and mature. The successful entrepreneur needs to recognize this and be willing to adjust and change his/her own management skills in order for the organization to reach its maximum potential.

Self-awareness through self-analysis is essential for the entrepreneur early in the process. Once a person is able to recognize and acknowledge his/her strengths and weaknesses, the odds of creating a successful entrepreneurial event go up significantly. The delicate balancing between soft and hard skills is not easy and, for some, not all that enjoyable. Those not cut out to manage an entity through various transitions will, hopefully, recognize this early and leave before a great concept goes awry.

There is nothing wrong with an entrepreneur launching events and then handing them off to let someone with different skills and interests grow it beyond his/her ability. The collective history of entrepreneurial events contains many examples of entrepreneurs who have done just that.

However, those who choose not to initiate multiple events and instead wish to build and grow one entity from scratch to maturity will reach an end-point and begin to wonder if there really is life outside of the business. This end-point may occur due to age or just becoming "burned-out" from years of responsibility and concentrated effort. The entrepreneur may wish to move on to that other career he/she has always thought about or there may be a desire to simply retire.

This also may be a point where new leadership in the organization might be just the thing to help ensure continued success.

Many entrepreneurs have gone on after spending nearly a lifetime at their entrepreneurial career to apply their creative talent in entirely new non-profit fields. An interesting website to peruse is www. purposeprize.org. This is a non-profit foundation called Civic Ventures that awards five $100,000 and 10, $10,000 prizes to people over the age of 50 to apply their entrepreneurial talent to address critical social problems at the local, regional or national level. In essence, they have left their for-profit careers and applied their talent to homelessness, social justice, human rights, violence, poverty, hunger, etc.

Here are some examples of award winners:

Ray Anderson founded a billion dollar carpet company called Interface, Inc. At the age of 60, he read Paul Hawken's book, The Ecology of Commerce and suddenly realized that some of the processes that he was using in his company were damaging the environment. He decided to work toward limiting his company's environmental footprint and, in so doing, became a public advocate, traveling the country and working with companies such as Wal-Mart and Boeing to assist them in reducing environmental impacts.

Anderson has developed ways and means to reduce emissions, water usage, energy use and landfill contributions. He stepped down from his company and is now giving 100 speeches a year while consulting with other corporations to assist in their environmental concerns.

Sixty-one-year-old, Robert Chambers stepped away from his car dealership and started a non-profit by the name of Bonnie CLAC (which stands for car loans and counseling). He has helped 750 people by training them in finance and then helping them find low-interest car loans. To date, only 17 of those who have gone through his program have failed to pay off their loan.

Martha Rollins, 63, started and built an antique store when she decided to go on to start a non-profit to provide job training for ex-convicts. Part of the training emphasizes how to start one's own business. Graduates of the program, with Rollins help, have started businesses such as a moving company and furniture restoration firm. Fifty-eight people have completed the program successfully.

Gene Jones, at the age of 84, after starting and acquiring a variety of businesses in a long career, founded the Opening Minds Through the Arts training program to bring the arts to K-8 students in the and around Tucson, Arizona. To date, more than 17,000 youngsters have enrolled in courses, which are now integrated into the curriculum. The program is expanding statewide and is credited with helping students significantly outscore their counterparts in other states on standardized testing. Two-thirds of parents report their children are doing better academically as a result of this program and 82 percent say their kids like school better. Jones says, "You sit on a shelf waiting for the billions of years this earth has been in existence, and you have your turn on stage for a nanosecond. To waste it by doing nothing is unthinkable."

While these examples demonstrate that there are numerous options for the entrepreneur after departing his/her company, there are other considerations. The entrepreneur first must weigh his/her own interests, the interests of the company and the interests of those who helped build this successful organization.

At this point, there are several choices. The company can be sold to key current employees, sold to another company or, at least in the "old" days, the entrepreneur could take the company public. Perhaps that day may come again. This is a decision that is personal and one that merits much thought and perhaps counsel from long-term mentors.

My Own Exit

I personally reached the point of departure in 1984. At the time, I was working as president of three different companies and finding myself increasingly worn out from over commitment. Our supermarket company had just come through a natural disaster in which three stores were flooded and one was totally destroyed. We took a nearly $1.5 million uninsured loss. Flooding occurred in 1978 and as we began to climb out of debt we were hit with high interest rates, but finally, by 1983, we had somewhat emerged from this time of turmoil.

I always harbored a desire to teach at the collegiate level. That year, the University of St. Thomas in St. Paul advertised an endowed position in entrepreneurship and small business. It was an intriguing opportunity and after much thought I did decide to apply. Part of the reason for the application was the pressure (encouragement) I received from my family. It seems that I spent too much time expounding about what I would teach in business school if given a chance and now they felt this was my opportunity to put up or shut up. I was offered the position and accepted it on one condition: the ability to work part-time for the first year while I sorted out the future of my businesses.

In two of my businesses, I was fortunate to have equity partners that were extremely competent - minimal participation was required on my part. Still, we needed to plan for less than minimal participation in the future. One of my business partners also wanted to retire and so we both agreed to sell. The other business had more partners, enough so that I would most likely not be missed all that much but the supermarkets, in which I was still deeply involved, presented a greater problem.

Since I was so involved in the grocery stores and did not really have top management to assume total control, I decided that I would need to sell. My biggest challenge was to make it happen before I started back to school in the fall and this was early summer. I decided to call one of my competitors and sat down and negotiated a win/win for the two of us. In the end, I decided to keep one store with some of my key employees. I then contributed 53 percent ownership through an Employee Stock Ownership Plan (E.S.O.P.) to about 55 employees.

In the negotiated sale for the other three stores, we decided that we would hire an independent third-party attorney to draft the sales agreement. The acquirer and I both felt that involving our own attorneys would take too much time and might even evolve into disagreement. Once drafted, since we both agreed to the terms, we took the agreement into a meeting with our attorneys present and explained what we had done. We told them they had two hours to review and, if they found no serious errors of omission, then we would sign. After a little consternation on the part of our attorneys everything went quite smoothly and the documents were signed.

From that point, I became an "education entrepreneur" and had a very enjoyable second career developing the entrepreneurial program at the University of St. Thomas over the next 13 years. I later went from St. Thomas to spend two years at the University of Iowa developing another program. From there, I eased into retirement by spending six years scouting and setting up investments for a venture-capital firm.

My own experience demonstrates that there is life after spending a career as an entrepreneur, building and developing a company. Exits can be handled successfully and the entrepreneur can go on and apply skills in other venues.

Final Departure

There are a variety of reasons one may wish to seek an exit strategy and these can include:

Family Issues

These can be anything from achieving an empty nest to a desire to travel.

Strategic Considerations

The firm is beginning to have difficulty competing

with new and growing competition and there is an advantageous marriage on the horizon that would assure continued growth and success.

Financial Considerations

The company needs a large reinvestment of capital and to do so would mean another round or risk at a time when thoughts have turned to retirement.

Management Needs

The company is short on talent in key positions. Attempts to fill the positions have not gone well.

Personal Issues

These can vary from a desire to retire to health issues.

Whatever the reason for contemplating an exit, the time has come to implement a harvesting and succession plan. It is a strange fact of life that few entrepreneurs ever consider it important enough to plan for the harvest early on in the life of the company. From personal experience, I can say that I was in this same camp but, everything becomes much more complicated and difficult later. Rather, if at the founding of the company, the entrepreneur has this conversation about exit considerations with close associates it will be easier to work through the issues later.

An exit strategy should be a long-term plan. Alternative strategies should be reviewed with key advisors, the board and legal counsel. The firm's value should be appraised periodically. The entrepreneur should think about what would be an acceptable price and terms. Constant surveillance will give indication of selling price within the industry as well as aid in developing a list of potential buyers.

So what should this early conversation with associates about harvesting consist of? First of all, each person should discuss the timeline they see for their involvement in the company. How long is each person willing to commit to the development? What are the expectations for everyone, particularly the entrepreneur's? If these matters are determined up front, it will save surprises down the road.

Secondly, it is important to think about what harvest will mean for the entrepreneur. Will it be totally cashing in, selling part interest and retaining a portion, merger with a larger entity, or a sale to a competitor? This plan does not necessarily have to be followed specifically 30 years down the road, but it will help determine the structure and development of the company.

I know of one entrepreneur who structured her company based on the desire to have it acquired by a major competitor. Throughout the development of the company, she studied and kept track of this competitor. She noted its acquisition criteria every time another company was purchased. She would network with the entrepreneur who had been acquired to find out what the buyer valued the most in the acquisition and made sure that she modeled her company accordingly. Fifteen years later, she sold her company to her target.

If the plan is to sell to internal management, then they must be developed, trained and educated to acquire the necessary skills to be effective managers after the current owner leaves. Training must to be part of planning early on as the requisite skill set may take years to acquire. Looking forward, this plan should also be taken into consideration during the hiring process.

Adopting the recommended open-book management system will make the transition of stepping away so much easier. I found that when we put our business in an E.S.O.P. 25 years ago, the shift in leadership was painless because key people already understood the financial statements and internal workings of the company. Of course the E.S.O.P. is another avenue for consideration as a vehicle for enabling a successful harvest.

Those considering an Employee Stock Ownership Plan (E.S.O.P) should first go online and visit www.

esopassociation.org, the website for the national organization for E.S.O.P. companies. This site has wonderful explanations of the ins and outs of creating an E.S.O.P. exit strategy. Since this is a federally approved vehicle administered by the IRS there are many legal requirements, which change on a fairly regular basis. In spite of the government red tape, there are extremely favorable tax considerations for the owner and the business. In addition, it offers a beneficial retirement vehicle for most company employees.

Those looking to sell to an outside investor, be it a group of employees or a strategic partner, will need a professional firm to complete a valuation in order to determine what the company might be worth. In my experience this number is usually a little less than what might have been hoped for but it does provide a basis from which to work. Value can be maximized if synergies with a strategic buyer can be found. Some firms are willing to pay a premium to eliminate a competitor.

Caution is advised when proceeding with a strategic buyer. Everything must eventually be disclosed, but shouldn't be disclosed too early in the discussion process. Ask for a non-disclosure agreement. I advise self-protection and remembering that it's not over until it's over. The entrepreneur should negotiate carefully; avoiding financing and earn-outs, if possible.

Chapter Ten

"Without the element of uncertainty, the bringing off of even the greatest business triumph would be a dull, routine and eminently unsatisfying affair."
J. Paul Getty

"In the beginning this seemed like a good idea"
"Is it possible to fail?"

I was hesitant to include this as a final chapter. After all no one goes into an entrepreneurial opportunity expecting to fail. Yet, even though the failure rate for new startups is considered high, in reality, it may not be much higher than the failure rate for a person in a new job.

Scott Shane, a professor of entrepreneurial studies at Case Western Reserve University, wrote a book titled, Illusions of Entrepreneurship: The Costly Myths that Entrepreneurs, Investors and Policy

Makers Live By (Yale University Press, 2008). Shane tabulates data from the Bureau of the Census and also from the Office of Advocacy of the U.S. Small Business Administration that shows failure rates to be considerably less than popularly believed.

Failure rates vary by a considerable margin, depending on the industry. The total starts from 1992 to 2002 show the average failure rate was about 71 percent, much lower than the widely held assumption of more than 90 percent Statistics aren't helpful to those who have failed but may provide some comfort for those starting out.

Charles Kettering once said, "An inventor fails 999 times, and if he succeeds once, he's in. He treats his failures simply as practice shots." There is much truth in this statement. Failure will always be a part of entrepreneurship, but how failure is handled is the greater test of personal ability.

A May 15, 2007 article in the Wall Street Journal by Melinda Beck titled, "If at First You Don't Succeed, You're in Excellent Company." focuses on successful people who suffered early failures. Twelve publishers originally turned down J. K. Rowling, the famous author of the Harry Potter series. Decca Records turned down the Beatles because they did not like their sound. Michael Jordan was cut from his high school basketball team.

Beck describes how some are able to recover from early failures - taking away lessons and working on those issues to finally achieve success. Psychologists call this "self-efficacy," or the unshakable belief that success will come. Self-efficacy differs from self-esteem because proponents of self-esteem often encourage people to adjust standards to a comfort level. In contrast, a high degree of self-efficacy demands continued high standards. The individual with high self-efficacy may, in fact, harbor low self-esteem feelings caused by repeated failures. Self-efficacy is described as a judgment of specific capabilities rather than a general feeling of self-worth.

Thomas Edison made 1,000 attempts before eventually succeeding with the development of the light bulb. Self-efficacy is a resilience that in some is like an inherent optimism. There is a great quote from Henry Ford that fits well: "Whether you think you can or you can't, you are usually right."

Passion also is vital for success. The entrepreneur should assess the amount of passion present for the endeavor being attempted. One technique that I used with people who were struggling to determine whether or not to start a particular business was to suggest they quit and show them alternative ideas that might be easier. If they would jump at the new suggestion, I knew that the passion was not there.

While failure is always a possibility, those energized by working with ambiguous situations, who have a passion for their pursuits and who can limit the amount of scar tissue events will greatly increase the odds of entrepreneurial success. Although I discussed earlier that some view the quality of the entrepreneur by the depth of his/her scar tissue, I certainly hope that this book offers insight about limiting both the amount and depth.

Risk is a part of the equation in an entrepreneurial event but does not need to be an overwhelming one. In an earlier chapter, I discussed ways and means to reduce risk and limit its impact. This is an important tactic that most successful entrepreneurs employ. Through reducing risk, one can most generally reach a level in harmony with risk tolerance. Risk then becomes a "calculated" one, understood from the start.

Age and circumstance will play a very important role in a personal analysis of inclination to risk failure. For the very young, there might be willingness to risk everything - youth allows time to recover from a total failure. For older entrepreneurs with families, assets and additional responsibilities such as a mortgage, the tolerance level will likely be much lower.

The book by Sarah Lacy, Once You're Lucky, Twice You're Good (Gotham Books, 2008) describes how many Silicon Valley entrepreneurs who had great initial successes have gone on to other startups - some are working but many are not. So often the circumstances can differ considerably between the different opportunities and very often people will confuse luck and timing with personal skill. I have always believed that the role that luck and timing play in success is too often discounted. Hitting a home run the first time at bat, may be due to luck and it would be unwise to claim home run batter status. On the other hand, luck can be defined as the place where preparation meets opportunity.

I had the good fortune to be personally involved with seven different startups in my business career, two of which were total failures. This helped me greatly to know and understand not only the process better but to also appreciate what others who are struggling might be going through.

Why Startups Fail

Wil Schroter is the founder and CEO of www. gobignetwork.com, a community of startup companies that share ideas online as well as offer relevant advice. They have conducted research on the pitfalls that trip up seemingly successful startup companies, but end up "flaming out" at a young age. The site identifies five key factors:

Lack of Focus

In my experience with literally hundreds of early stage companies I would have to say that this is one that stands head and shoulders above any other reason for failure. The entrepreneurial mindset is such that personality is recharged through new challenge. The onset of this condition can be precipitated by too much early success and, thus, looking around for the next elephant to slay. It also can come about as boredom sets in due to a more predictable routine. One should not ignore new opportunity, but true stability with the nucleus of the company is vital. The focus should be to hone that initial idea to absolute perfection. This takes time, effort and focus! The entrepreneur must stick to core competencies and keep it simple. Al Ries the author of, Focus: The Future of Your Company Depends On It, (Harper Business, 1996) reinforces this concept with examples of Dell Computer and Best Buy. These two companies polished their central idea to perfection becoming better than any competitor. When extraneous opportunities begin to consume time, distraction will certainly make it easier to stumble. A general rule to follow is to stay focused on anything that will help gain customers, keep customers or improve service.

Meager (or inadequate/poorly executed) Marketing

Marketing, in a sense, is the front side of selling. The message the public sees about any product/service must be carefully managed. Consistency is key here. Quality and impeccable service must be conveyed in even the smallest detail. I recently read about a new Lexus dealership that cost the owner $35 million to build. The new showroom features polished tile and leather lounge chairs, some of which vibrate. Valet parking greets customers, followed by an escort from the concierge to the coffee bar, featuring fresh baked sweet goods. This dealership is "marketing" a luxury car with a consistent message of quality and prestige. New dealership sales have almost tripled over the previous, more normal location, where plastic chairs and a self-serve aluminum coffee urn with day old coffee welcomed the potential buyer.

Cash Management

I have touched on this previously, but feel it is so essential that it bears repeating. My grandfather had a "cash drawer" in his office, which was monitored at least twice a day. I believe that to be an important lesson. Cash is the lifeblood of a business. There is nothing more important to achieving sustainability than the careful and deliberate oversight of cash. It is more important to have regular and timely cash flow statements than P & L and Balance Sheet statements. In my own businesses, where I no longer have day-to-day operating responsibility, the first question I ask my managers is always, "How is the cash flow?" If it is growing, things are generally okay.

Cramped Trigger Finger

Efficient decision-making is critical. People expect quick and timely decisions from the person in charge. In entrepreneurial endeavors, there will not always be time to send issues to a committee for study. This means that decisions will, at times, need to be made unilaterally with limited information. Others should still be used as a sounding board in decision-making, but ultimately, the "buck stops" with the owner/ CEO. Procrastination will seldom help and in fact, many times, can make a situation worse. It is often better to make a decision and amend it later than to wait too long.

Poor Execution

It is critical that time to delivery of the product or service is always ASAP. Speed is essential and needs to come before perfection of product. Reputation for speedy order fulfillment in today's world is an important attribute for any company. I buy and read many books each year and also tend to purchase books for family and friends as gifts. This year my favorite online bookstore has allowed its normal speedy service to slip drastically. Books I ordered for Christmas gifts in early November were not delivered until after Christmas. That is totally unacceptable and they managed to lose me as a customer. Whatever is sold, be it a product or a service, an array of steps needs to occur between the time the order is given and the customer receives the final product/service. Each step should be assessed to be sure that it is fulfilled with the greatest proficiency and efficiency possible. Associates should not be burdened with too many "rules and policies" when it comes to order fulfillment. Being known for superior execution is one of the better competitive advantages one can have.

Personal Reflections

From my own experience in dealing with both personal failures and those I have witnessed through students, I can add some additional lessons and advice to the list above. This list represents my personal scar tissue.

Know the Business

· Endeavors which one knows nothing about should be avoided.

· Whenever possible, volunteer as an apprentice to learn more.

· Team members should have in-depth experience in the industry.

· Significant investment should be avoided until one is comfortable with his/her own industry knowledge.

Accountability

· Proper checks and balances always need to be maintained.

· Accurate and timely records, measurements and reporting systems are essential.

· Do monthly cash flow analysis with a rolling six-month projection.

· Irresponsibility with company money can never be tolerated.

Avoid Constantly Testing Limits

· Limit excessive risk taking.

· Take calculated risks and utilize risk reduction strategies.

· Do not become overly enamored with a first success (luck and timing do play a role).

· Try not to "bet the farm" too often.

Don't Wait Until It Is Too Late to Take Action

· Confront problems early.

· Problems do not solve themselves.

·Doing something is usually better than doing nothing.

· Wrong decisions can generally be corrected.

Product-Market Structure

· Avoid markets that are overwhelmingly large or too small to achieve significance.

· Avoid a product or service that is easily duplicated by competition.

· Avoid features of the product or service that can be served by similar products or the combination of similar products.

Be Aware of Competitive Dynamics

· Overpowering competition.

· High cost of entry.

· Inability to expand beyond one product or service.

Business Economics to Watch Out For

· Overwhelming financial requirements.

· Inability to produce quantities competitively.

· Lack of influence and control over inputs.

· Inability to harvest.

Remember Always

· Those who obsess about the possibility of failure seldom achieve success.

As much as I would like to say that this is an all-encompassing list, it is not. There will always be the unknown - things that seemingly come from nowhere. Anyone can suddenly find him/herself staring failure in the face. When one of my students found himself in this situation - caused by a dominant customer who suddenly did not renew a contract - he froze. He finally called me and asked me what to do. I asked what he had been doing and it turned out that he had essentially locked himself in his office and was doing nothing.

I asked this student what he done in the early days to win customers. He replied that he had virtually called everyone he could think of who might need his service. This call, if the potential customer was close to making a decision, was often followed by a visit. I asked him to just stop and think about that for a minute, if it worked at the start, why not now? He took this limited advice and got back to work and eventually salvaged his company through maximizing his sales effort, successfully selling a few years later.

In my own case, the reader may recall the story I shared in Chapter One, I was hit with a natural disaster right after having seven successful record years. I thought we were on a roll. We had dominant market share in our area and things were great. Then suddenly, they were not.

When unexpected crisis strikes, I believe that everything humanly possible should be done to affect change. I remember walking around the block after my initial confrontation with the banker who refused to extend any more credit (this came after he had promised to stand behind us during our recovery. I guess he thought that applied to moral not financial support) and after a long conversation with myself, I thought we had come too far to walk away. I was determined to not let failure happen, even if I had to will it not to happen. Of course, it took a little audacity to walk into the competing bank, but I knew in my heart that if we could get over this hump we could crawl back to more successful days, which we did.

It is difficult for any entrepreneur to admit that the venture might not be a success. There may come a time when one must stop pouring resources and time into a failed concept. At this point, as it was when the business first got off the ground, it is important to find "mentors" who can provide an objective opinion. It is better to seek outside counsel to make sure that this might be the time to burn a bridge and walk away. Remember, one can always start another venture.

Throughout this book, I have attempted to share some scar tissue to help the budding entrepreneur develop opportunity. There are lessons to be learned from those who have gone before. There is no need to reinvent the wheel. Hopefully, the lessons presented here will make life a little easier.

I always taught a capstone course for the entrepreneurial program which closed with the following 10 bits of wisdom for final consideration.

· Things go down faster than they go up.

· Problems come in bunches.

· First reactions are usually right.

· When in doubt—check the grapevine.

· If it doesn't feel right—it usually is not.

· It never hurts to sleep on a decision before implementation.

· The best way around a problem is always through it.

· Measure competencies of people by overall results—not the small things.

· Learn from the mistakes of others—you can never live long enough to make them all yourself.

· Enthusiasm, loyalty and devotion of the heart, mind and soul cannot be bought by any man. These must be earned.

· Oh yes, I forgot the most important one of all: NEVER, EVER RUN OUT OF CASH!

CARPE

DIEM

About the Author

Daryl Erdman has more than 40 years experience in business development and entrepreneurial education.

He began his career in the family grocery store business in the early 1960s and later greatly expanded his experience through launching a number of start ups, pioneering entrepreneurial education programs at both the University of St. Thomas and the University of Iowa and assisting in the launch of a number of other companies through work in the venture capital industry.

His professional experience includes: serving for six years as senior director of AAVIN Venture Capital, a $47 million Small Business Investment Company leveraged venture fund; working for two years (1996-1998) as director of the John Pappajohn Entrepreneurial Center at the University of Iowa; developing a 22-course entrepreneurial program in entrepreneurship which included a minor for the University of Iowa College of Engineering; developing the entrepreneurship program at the University of St. Thomas in St. Paul, Minnesota(1983-96); while serving as endowed chair in Small Business and Entrepreneurship and director for the Center for Entrepreneurship at the University of St. Thomas.

The University of Iowa program he helped develop was recognized in a March 1998 Inc. Magazine cover story. The St. Thomas entrepreneurial program was ranked 13th in a ranking of the top 25 collegiate entrepreneurial programs by Success magazine in 1995. The University of Iowa program was listed in the top 35 in 1998.

The author's entrepreneurial experience includes: president of Midwest Taco (two stores); president of Erdman's Supermarkets, Inc (seven stores); founder and president of Rotab Corp. (12 restaurants), founder of Aldeen's Menswear and Tie Rack, Inc.; and a founder and treasurer of Mems Technology (a medical device company). He was actively involved in developing a radio network, weekly newspaper, trading stamp company, temporary employment agency as well as residential and commercialproperty development. He has served on the board of several early-stage companies and was on the Board of Regents at Luther College. He remains active in two of his own companies, serving as board chair.

Professional associations include: serving for three years as OMNI, a statewide-certified development corporation and seven years on the national Advisory Board of the U.S. Small Business Administration. He was a founder and chairman of Metro Development, a private, non-profit certified development corporation; currently ranked third in the nation with a $450 million small business loan portfolio. He also was a member of the board and chaired the business development subcommittee of Minnesota Project Innovation.

Erdman has been the recipient of a number of business awards and acknowledgements. He was awarded the National Federation of Independent Business Foundation honor for entrepreneurial education curriculum design. Both entrepreneurial programs he helped develop won the National Model Program Award from the U.S. Association of Small Business and Entrepreneurship. In 1993, the author was recognized by the Kaufmann Foundation's Center for Entrepreneurial Leadership as one of the top 10 innovators in entrepreneurship education in the nation. He also was named as a finalist in 1994 in the Ernst & Young Entrepreneur of the Year Program in the Supporter of Entrepreneurship category.

He received his bachelor of arts degree in business and mathematics from Luther College, located in Decorah, Iowa and his MBA from Michigan State University. He also studied entrepreneurship at Babson College in Boston as a Price-Babson Fellow. In 1987, he received the Babson's Edwin M. Appel award for bringing entrepreneurial vitality to academia.

The author currently resides near Grand Rapids, Minnesota with Audrey, his wife of 48 years. The couple has six grandchildren who enjoy many visits to "the lake." Winters are spent snowmobiling and skiing, while summers are spent boating and sailing.